THE OPEN BOOK SERIES

THE ANCIENT GREEKS & ROMANS

Edited by Jane Reid

Crete – Europe's First Civilisation – the Greek Miracle – the Greeks in the Mediterranean – the Greatest Greek – the Greek Genius – the Birth of Rome – the Roman Republic – Rome at War – the Golden Era of Imperial Rome

HODDER AND STOUGHTON
LONDON SYDNEY AUCKLAND TORONTO

British Library Cataloguing in Publication Data

Reid, Jane
    The ancient Greeks and Romans. – (The open
book series)
    1. Civilization, Greek – Juvenile literature
    2. Rome – Civilization – Juvenile literature
    I. Title
    938   DF79

    ISBN 0-340-33691-9 (Cased)
    ISBN 0-340-32900-9 (Pbk)

Copyright © 1981 Gruppo Editoriale Fabbri S.p.A.,
Milano – Le Livre de Paris S.A. – Hachette,
Bagneux.

English language edition copyright © 1984
Hodder and Stoughton Ltd.

First published in this edition in Great Britain 1984.
Second impression 1984

Published by Hodder and Stoughton Children's Books,
a division of Hodder and Stoughton Ltd, Mill Road,
Dunton Green, Sevenoaks, Kent TN13 2YJ.

Photoset by Rowland Phototypesetting Ltd,
Bury St Edmunds, Suffolk.

Printed in Belgium by Henri Proost et Cie,
Turnhout.

Crete: Europe's First Civilisation

After fifty years of Greek rule the Cretan people revolted. The rebels invaded the courtyard of the palace at Knossos. Fire began to eat into the wooden columns which supported the upper chambers. Salvation could only come from the intervention of the gods. Wearing the ceremonial robes of the deposed Cretan monarchs, the foreign king prepared for the sacred ceremony. By the fountain in the throne room the holy water was made ready, to wash away their sins and cause divine favour to fall once again upon the king. The king never reached the water of expiation. The beams supporting the ceiling cracked; the columns crumbled. With a roar, the ceiling and the upper floors fell in, burying everything in layers of rubble. It was the late spring of a year around 1400 B.C.

Plan of the Royal Palace of Knossos:
1. Central Courtyard: 2. North Entrance and House of the Bodyguard:
3. Storehouses: 4. Antechamber to the Throne Room: 5. Throne Room: 6. Corridor joining the Sanctuary and the Crypt:
7. Peristyle and Stairway to the Royal Chambers: 8. The Queen's Apartment:
9. Main Staircase: 10. Southern Pillars:
11. Southern Entrance: 12. Theatre Area.

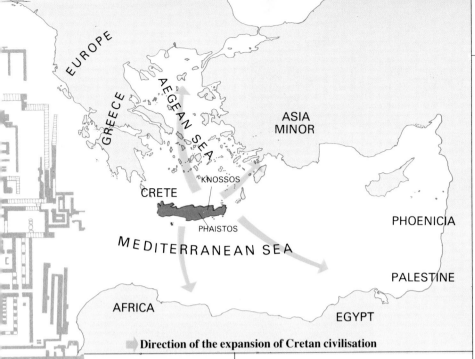

Direction of the expansion of Cretan civilisation

A MARITIME EMPIRE

Between 2500 and 2000 B.C., metal fever exploded. Gold, silver and above all the tin and copper necessary to the making of bronze began to be the most prized merchandise available, from Egypt to Greece and from Italy to Mesopotamia.

It was because of this that Crete's long and magical era dawned. She was not an island rich in minerals but she possessed ships; ships which sailed throughout the Mediterranean.

To foreign ports these ships carried oil, wine, grain, painted vases and products made in the Cretan foundries by Cretan artisans. And in exchange they carried away loads of tin and copper and bronze ingots which were then either reshaped at home, or resold to make huge profits.

Within a few decades the Cretans had created a vast maritime empire for themselves. Naturally enough, the wealth this created had, on occasion, to be protected by force at sea. All the ships, in fact, were well armed and 'merchant-seamen' were able to transform themselves instantly into warriors and even, on occasion, into pirates.

For centuries no nation risked contesting maritime supremacy with the Cretan fleet: her dominion over the waves was so complete that the simple presence of her ships was enough to assure complete protection for the wealthy cities of the island.

THE LABYRINTH OF KNOSSOS

The Cretan cities which had the best natural harbours naturally grew to be the richest and strongest. Even amongst these, Knossos was quickly dominant and it soon became the capital of the island. The kings of Knossos had as their emblem the 'labrys' – the double-headed axe which had once been a weapon of war and then became an instrument in the city's religious ceremonies.

Just as the symbol of the 'labrys' flew high on the flags around the royal residence, so the palace became identified with it and finally 'the palace of the Labrys' became known simply as the 'labyrinth'. It was an extremely complex structure. Over the years, different floors, rooms, stairways, passages, piazzas, warehouses and a variety of new rooms were added to the original edifice.

The royal palace was situated at the heart of the territory pertaining to Knossos. All around the palace the king owned huge warehouses in which the Cretans accumulated oil, wine, grain, tin, copper and bronze for working or for resale. In the midst of these, all around the great paved courtyard, rose the many small workshops of the Cretan artisans: vasemakers, craftsmen, engravers, and artists of every type.

The market was also held here and on the major holidays, the great religious festivals which culminated in musical or theatrical spectaculars or great sporting competitions.

THE PROOF

Three thousand three hundred years later – in the April of A.D. 1900 – the English scholar, Arthur Evans, digging amidst the ruins of the palace of Knossos, brought to light the evidence which testifies to the fact that this ceremony was so tragically interrupted.

The revolt of the Cretans against their foreign masters (futile because they did not succeed in removing them) and the destruction of the magnificent royal palace signalled the beginning of the last act in the story of Crete and the end of the first great civilisation in Europe, which had begun almost five thousand years ago.

THE ADVANTAGES OF CRETE'S POSITION

Crete is an island of fairly modest dimensions in the eastern Mediterranean. It is 260 kilometres in length, and its breadth varies between 12 and 56 kilometres. The original inhabitants of the island probably reached it some time around the year 6000 B.C., arriving from the coasts of present-day Turkey and Lebanon.

For three thousand and more years they lived there isolated and in peace. Villages and cities, which were effectively independent, prospered with their agriculture (olives, vines, fruit and wheat), by raising cows and sheep, and by fishing, and also through maritime commerce with neighbouring islands.

Their ships, which were built with wood taken from the forests which were then widespread in the mountainous zones, were powered by oars and by sail. To sail from one island to another became easy for them. By day, there was always a mountain peak or the outline of a known coast in sight to indicate the position in which the ship found herself. By night, there was always the shore and nearby land on which to rest in safety until the dawn. The experience of centuries, moreover, had taught the Cretans the ancient eastern methods of navigation by the sun and the stars: from island to island as far as Greece and from there the 'great leap' as far as the south of Italy, or perhaps towards the east as far as the coast of Lebanon, from there to follow the shoreline to Egypt.

It was really the fortunate geographical position of Crete, at the centre of the trade routes between three different continents, which settled the splendid destiny of the island.

While all about him fire raged and the rebels invaded his courtyards, the Cretan king calmly prepared to perform a sacred invocatory rite to the gods.

THE BULL: A SACRED SYMBOL

The bull was the emblem of Minoan Cretan civilisation. The animal was venerated as a symbol of strength, and fertility. Archaeological remains from Cretan sites have shown that the bull was represented on many decorative objects. The vase illustrated above was probably used to hold oil and wine necessary in religious sacrifices.

SACRED GAMES

Whenever there was a religious holiday, the Cretan people would flock to the courtyard in front of the palace at Knossos, or, if that was too far for them, to some convenient large space where sacrifice would be made to the gods. Once this offering had been made and the sacrificial rites were ended, the games would begin. They were participated in by the young men, in honour of the gods. Such games spread to Greece and later became the model for the Olympics.

The Cretans loved races, boxing, wrestling and armed combat, but there was one particular sport, and a particularly dangerous one, that they loved above all: bull jumping. Young men would mount the backs of angry bulls, at great risk to their own lives, and attempt to do acrobatic feats on the bull, in much the same way as a circus acrobat performs tricks on the back of a horse. Naturally this enraged the bull. When the acrobat had finished his attempts to entertain the crowds, the bull, excited to the point of frenzy, and enraged at the noise and the dazzling colours all around him, would put his head down and charge. That was when the fun began. Young men, and young women, too, would attempt to jump over its back as it charged. After these spectacular and foolhardy jumps, they would then try to pull the frenzied animal to the ground, where it was killed.

A DIFFERENT RELIGION

Unlike all the other peoples of the Mediterranean, the Cretans did not build grand temples and altars to glorify and worship their gods.

The islanders of Crete worshipped their gods not as dead beings but as living things – in woods, in caves and grottoes, at the sources of streams and rivers and at the summits of mountains.

According to Cretan legend, the father of all the gods lived on the majestic Mount Ida, at the centre of the island.

The Cretan religion was very simple. The people worshipped the natural phenomena that they saw all around them and which manifested themselves in a wide variety of ways. For example, the vitality of the bull, the beauty of the lilies in the field, the joy of watching a bird soar overhead; all of these symbols, and many more, were often represented in Cretan paintings, sculptures, carvings and, indeed, even on the king's crown.

A fresco from the royal palace at Knossos, showing a youth doing a somersault on a bull's back.

Above: A cup used during religious ceremonies. Right: A decorated glass.

CRETAN ART

The work of the Cretan engravers and potters was famous throughout the entire Mediterranean. Jewels, vases, bronze objects and other artefacts of the Cretan craftsmen have been found in many archaeological digs throughout the island. Here are several important examples.

The Mysterious Mother Earth

The supreme divinity of the Cretan religion was Mother Earth, from whom all goodness came. She symbolised life, fertility and the cycle of life from birth to death, and eventual rebirth. She is usually represented standing tall, in ceremonial robes, her arms outstretched to welcome those who come to worship her, and with her breasts bare to give nourishment to those who need it.

In some paintings, Mother Earth is shown to hold two serpents symbolising underworld life and the existence of the afterlife.

THE PRINCE OF LILIES

A young Cretan prince carries out a sacrificial rite during the festival of springtime. As a symbol of his authority he wears a curious crown made of red lilies. The painting above, found in the palace of Knossos, is known by that name – the Prince of the Lilies.

THE MYSTERIOUS WRITING

Although we know a great deal about life on Crete from the numerous objects that have been found there – scenes painted on the walls of the royal palace, or on cups and vases and pots, not just in Crete but also in nearby Egypt – most of our knowledge of Cretan life comes from the last of their systems of writing that they used – the only one of the four so far to be decoded.

Among the writings found on Crete, the most mysterious is the hieroglyphics used there between 2000 and 1600 B.C. This system used a series of pictorial signs similar to those used by the Egyptians. There are two forms of this hieroglyphic writing:

Linear A uses signs that probably indicate the sounds of the syllables. It has not been decoded.

Linear B is the only one of the forms of writing that has been decoded. The signs use the same words as Ancient Greek, but in Cretan writing. It was only in use in Knossos after 1450 B.C., that is to say, after the conquest of the island by people from the Greek mainland.

GRANDEUR AND DECLINE

Crete was at the height of its civilisation around 2000 B.C. During the four centuries before that she had consolidated her maritime supremacy and was trading all around the eastern Mediterranean Sea. The three

Gold pendant

Gold cup

centuries after 2000 B.C. saw her continue in this advantageous position.

However, the history of the island is dominated by catastrophes about which we know very little. Around about 1700 B.C. an earthquake seems to have destroyed the royal palaces. (It may have been an invasion of Achaeans from the Greek mainland that was responsible. We do not know.)

However, the Cretans rebuilt their palaces on an even larger scale than before – and Cretan colonists began to settle on Greek islands. Civilisation on Crete was booming again during the seventeenth and sixteenth centuries B.C. and exercised a strong influence on the more backward culture of mainland Greece. Around 1500 to 1450 B.C. another catastrophe or series of catastrophes occurred. Some of the damage must have been done by the volcanic eruption on the island of Thera which virtually exploded and may have caused a tidal wave of such dimensions that many of the palaces were destroyed and not rebuilt.

Even if the tidal wave did not do as much damage as some people think, it was followed by a more serious disaster. Weakened by the effects of the Thera volcano, the Cretans could not withstand invasion by marauding Greeks, and by 1450 B.C. Knossos was under the control of these Greeks. The shattered palaces elsewhere on the island were not rebuilt.

Around 1400 B.C. another catastrophe ended the Greek presence, but the distinctive Cretan culture never recovered. The future lay with the Greeks on the mainland.

Our knowledge of Cretan society at this time comes mainly from the surviving fragments of the bright, cheerful frescoes that were executed in a vividly expressive, cartoon-like style; and from statuettes, plaster reliefs, painted pottery and stones carved for use as seals.

In paintings, the people seem to have been relaxed and attractive men and women. The men stride about wearing only loincloths and boots. The women wear well-made tunics with little puff sleeves, and their faces are quite heavily made up.

One interesting feature is that the soldiers do not appear to have worn body armour until Cretan society was definitely in decline.

The Greek Miracle

Between the years 2000 and 1200 B.C. new peoples from the prairies of southern Russia and from the lands along the Danube flooded into two continents – they spread into India and all over Europe. But it was in Greece they were to make the greatest impression. Having conquered the country, little by little they gave birth to a civilisation of such importance for humanity that many historians speak of a genuine 'Greek Miracle'. At the root of this miracle, we find cities such as Argos, Tiryns, Mycenae . . . above all, Mycenae, the proof of its extraordinary civilisation given by the treasures (precious jewels and golden artefacts) discovered in the tombs of its kings thousands of years later by the German archaeologist, Heinrich Schliemann . . .

THE MAIN CHARACTERS IN A NEW ERA OF HISTORY

Who were these characters who, in reality, turned over a new page in history? We can tell from fragments that they identified themselves by different names according to their ethnic groups or popular allegiances. Modern historians put them all together into a single ethnic category – based on their origins and, more so, on their diffusion – and they are described as Indo-Europeans. They are, in effect, our direct ancestors. Right up until the long-past agricultural revolution, the centre of human civilisation (not, of course, forgetting the great contributions made by India and China) was the Near East and more specifically the area from Egypt to Mesopotamia. In this new era the centre of civilisation moved from the confines of the imperial and agrarian eastern empires to the green islands and the dynamic mercantile cities of the Eastern Mediterranean. Above all it moved into Europe, and to be more precise, into Greece, to the Indo-European tribes of the Achaeans.

A precise division of duties

The first invaders of Greece came with metal armour, bronze weapons and, to make victory even more certain, a few war chariots. So they easily defeated entire villages of virtually unarmed peasants.

It was thus that groups of a few hundred Achaean warriors were able to subjugate the local population and impose themselves as overlords.

In the different cities, allied to each other but independent, kings installed themselves and their military chiefs with their loyal warriors. They did not reduce the conquered populace to a state of complete slavery, but instead established a precise division of duties. The king and his 'noble' warriors had to govern the city and its surrounding countryside and, should the need arise, they had to take up arms to defend the city and its inhabitants.

On fixed dates and according to an established rate, the shepherds paid their dues to the king and his court, in animals to be killed for meat and the supply of unbleached wool for clothes and trade.

The farmers brought grain, vegetables, wine and above all, olive oil, to the king's warehouses. Craftsmen and workers yielded to the king objects for everyday use and for use in bartering with foreign merchants.

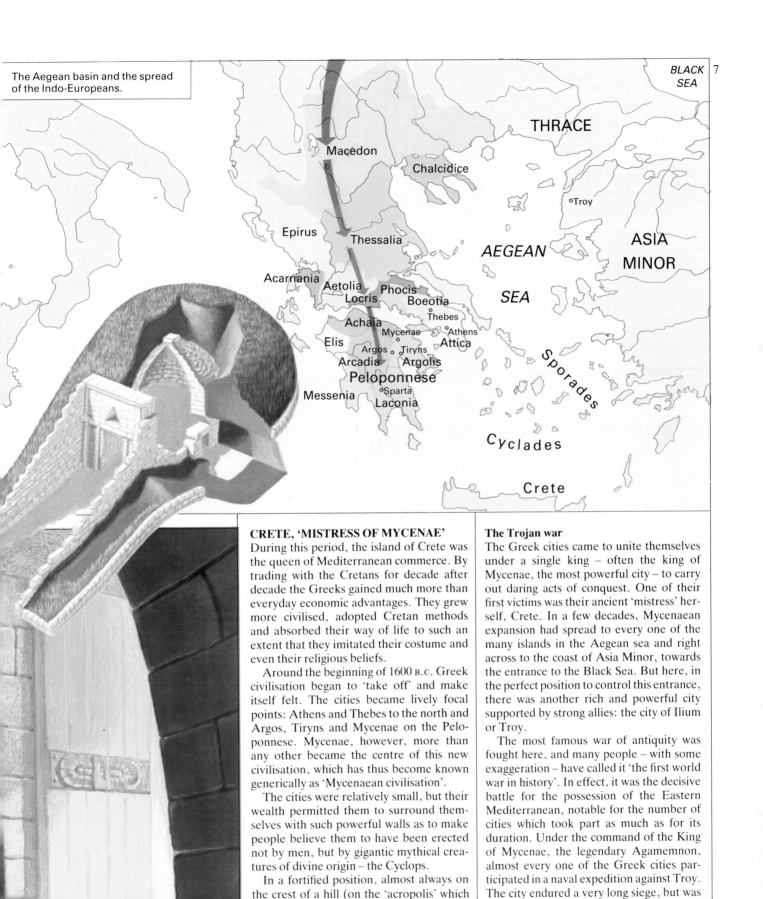

The Aegean basin and the spread of the Indo-Europeans.

THRACE

Macedon

Chalcidice

°Troy

Epirus

Thessalia

AEGEAN

ASIA MINOR

SEA

Acarnania

Aetolia

Phocis

Locris

Boeotia

Thebes °

Achaïa

Mycenae °

°Athens

Elis

Argos ° ° Tiryns

Attica

Arcadia

Argolis

Peloponnese

Sporades

Messenia

°Sparta

Laconia

Cyclades

Crete

CRETE, 'MISTRESS OF MYCENAE'

During this period, the island of Crete was the queen of Mediterranean commerce. By trading with the Cretans for decade after decade the Greeks gained much more than everyday economic advantages. They grew more civilised, adopted Cretan methods and absorbed their way of life to such an extent that they imitated their costume and even their religious beliefs.

Around the beginning of 1600 B.C. Greek civilisation began to 'take off' and make itself felt. The cities became lively focal points: Athens and Thebes to the north and Argos, Tiryns and Mycenae on the Peloponnese. Mycenae, however, more than any other became the centre of this new civilisation, which has thus become known generically as 'Mycenaean civilisation'.

The cities were relatively small, but their wealth permitted them to surround themselves with such powerful walls as to make people believe them to have been erected not by men, but by gigantic mythical creatures of divine origin – the Cyclops.

In a fortified position, almost always on the crest of a hill (on the 'acropolis' which means the 'high point of the city'), rose the royal palace. This was a veritable citadel with many rooms, courtyards, stables and warehouses. On the acropolis also stood the great tombs like the so-called Treasury of Atreus at Mycenae (reconstructed cross-section shown above) which each king had built to house himself after his death.

The Trojan war

The Greek cities came to unite themselves under a single king – often the king of Mycenae, the most powerful city – to carry out daring acts of conquest. One of their first victims was their ancient 'mistress' herself, Crete. In a few decades, Mycenaean expansion had spread to every one of the many islands in the Aegean sea and right across to the coast of Asia Minor, towards the entrance to the Black Sea. But here, in the perfect position to control this entrance, there was another rich and powerful city supported by strong allies: the city of Ilium or Troy.

The most famous war of antiquity was fought here, and many people – with some exaggeration – have called it 'the first world war in history'. In effect, it was the decisive battle for the possession of the Eastern Mediterranean, notable for the number of cities which took part as much as for its duration. Under the command of the King of Mycenae, the legendary Agamemnon, almost every one of the Greek cities participated in a naval expedition against Troy. The city endured a very long siege, but was only finally captured – so it is said – because of the unfair tactics of Ulysses, King of Ithaca.

Troy was taken, completely destroyed, and burnt to the ground. The Eastern Mediterranean and the rich coasts of Asia Minor were in the indisputable possession of the Greeks.

8 THE BIRTH OF THE 'POLIS' AND THE POWER OF SPARTA

The civilisation of Mycenae had a relatively short life-span. There, between 1200 and 1100 B.C., began a new Indo-European invasion flooding over Central Greece and the Peloponnese.

The Doric invasion

The invaders were the Dorians, whose iron weapons shattered – sometimes literally – the resistance of the Mycenaean's bronze weapons.

The entire country descended into a 'dark age' about which we know very little and which lasted for about four centuries.

This epoch was characterised by the movement of various peoples towards Asia Minor and by the formation of the political body which was to typify ancient Greece: the 'polis' or 'city state'. The entire history of Greece is the history of these states, particularly the two most powerful of them all: Sparta and Athens.

Sparta was the most famous and powerful city of the Dorians and for a period succeeded in dominating the whole of Greece.

Power in the hands of a few

The Mycenaean sovereigns, who were ousted by the Dorians, were kings of great renown: rulers, judges, lawmakers, overseers, high priests. All power was effectively in their hands.

The Dorians, too, recognised the supremacy of a single leader, but almost exclusively only in times of war.

After the conquest the land was divided, along with the spoils of war and the subject peoples, into more or less equal parts for each king. It is easy to understand how, in this way, the power of the king was reduced little by little.

As far as wealth was concerned, the king had no more than the other prominent warrior landowners who fought at his side in times of war. In battle, however, one man's strength and courage could be used to inspire others.

In times of peace, on the other hand, all major decisions were taken with the consent of all these potentates, who were seen as 'equals'.

In the different cities, the governing power was steadily removed from the king. At the most, he was recognised as having the right to preside over religious ceremonies and the assemblies of the 'equals'.

The Assembly – the gathering of the heads of the most influential families – was the real governing force in the various cities. The system was called an 'aristocracy' (government by the élite, by the privileged) or perhaps, 'oligarchy' (a government whose power is in the hands of a few people). It was the first step in a great development.

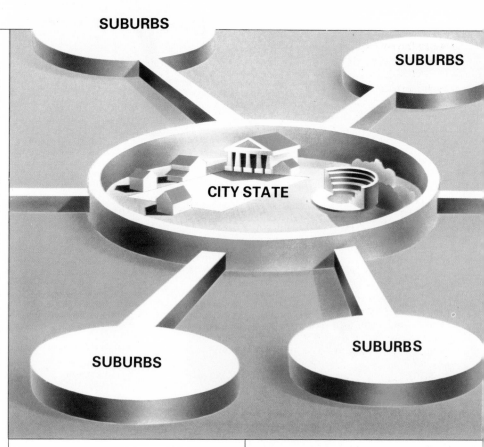

From equals to equals

In ancient Greece, what was important was not only the actual city itself, but, as we can see from the diagram above, there was also its territory. For this reason we talk of city-states. In the 'demi' themselves (the villages surrounding the centre of population), were found the properties of the most powerful of the citizens. Moreover, the fact that one was an inhabitant did not mean one was a citizen. In the territory of a polis, there also lived slaves who had no rights at all and also foreigners who were free to work and, in the end, to fight. But the 'true' citizens were those born of the free native population of the polis: at the outset, they consisted only of the nobles and the very wealthy.

Every so often they would meet at the 'agora', the square in the middle of the polis where the temples and public buildings were sited. During these assemblies they would discuss, as equals, all the matters which concerned the community and would also elect amongst themselves those who were to serve in this position of power – the magistrates – who generally served for a year at a time.

THE GOVERNMENT OF SPARTA

Even during the most intense periods of development in Sparta, there were never more than 5,000 recognised as true citizens. To these we must add around 10,000 people who had no political standing – these were the wives, the children and the dependants of the citizens.

About a further 200,000 bonded servants and slaves were their subjects. Amongst the 5,000 citizens there existed a certain balance and equality. Amongst themselves they addressed each other as 'equals'. The Assembly of the Equals (the Apella) nominated a council of 28 members: the ancients or elders who took all the most important decisions. The Apella then elected five superintendents, the efori (who corresponded roughly to the ministers of today) and two kings who took control of the armed forces. This arrangement was so strongly adhered to that it earned several centuries of stability for the Spartan state.

Sparta, the Dorian capital

Sparta was the ideal site for an important polis. It stood on the banks of the River Eurota, beneath green hills, dominated by Mount Taigets, in the centre of a fertile plain. The area, however, was already inhabited but the Dorians did not hesitate to take it.

With force of arms they crushed those who dared to resist them, and they kept their descendants in a perpetual state of slavery. These people were the Helots (from the village of Helos). Their fate was to toil in the small villages to support their conquerors. They had no civil rights at all, and whenever necessary were requisitioned by the army as auxiliary troops.

There were also people who had not had the courage to oppose the Dorian invaders. These people were granted the right to live near Sparta and carry on their business. They were known as 'Perieci', or those who live on the outskirts. They were 'semi-free' because they were useful, but they had absolutely no say at all in the government. Finally, there were the descendants of the victorious Dorian invaders themselves. They officially described themselves as 'Spartiati', the 'true Spartans', the only citizens in possession of full rights.

The military training of hoplite Spartans. In open air, in a type of 'war arena', groups of hoplites armed to the teeth engage in simulated hand-to-hand fighting.

A great military academy

For the 'true' young Spartan – the 'equal' of the future – there was only one aim: to become a skilled warrior.

The Spartan 'opliti' (hoplites), the ranks of the infantrymen armed to the teeth who fought side by side to form a wall of iron and sword, were the greatest fighters in the world at that time.

Their education commenced as soon as their infancy ended. At the age of seven they were taken from their families and educated in state military academies until they reached adulthood. Humiliation, exhaustion, and rigid daily military exercising produced one of two results: either the young man 'dropped out' and was forbidden all civil rights and expelled from the community of 'true' Spartiati feared by all who fought against them, or he became a warrior of exceptional quality.

At the age of thirty, he was finally permitted to conduct his own business. For his entire life, however, he was never to forget that he was, above all else, a soldier. It was his duty to stay in prime physical condition and fitness and never to forget the meals he shared with his fellow warriors. These meals were always the same, unpleasant 'black soup' made from the blood and meat of a pig, seasoned with salt and vinegar, with added vegetables.

ATHENS AND THE BIRTH OF DEMOCRACY

To an educated person today, the idea of Athens immediately brings to mind some of the greatest works of human genius: art, poetry, theatre . . . These are, of course, important, but Athens altered ancient history in another way; it was there that was born the modern idea of democracy. (The Greek word *demokratia* means government by the people.)

A good place to be

The Indo-Europeans who, in the distant past, occupied Attica and founded the city of Athens, belonged to the 'family' of the Ionians. Of the three natural elements which shaped the destiny of this most famous city, we should probably examine only the first initially. This was its location – easy to defend on a hill and dominating the largest and most fertile plain in Greece after that of Sparta.

The other two favourable elements were realised only after technical and economic developments made it possible. The first was the abundance of ideal natural ports along the coast, exemplified by the two most accessible natural ports on the doorstep of Athens, Piraeus and Phalerum. The other was the silver mines on nearby Mount Laurion which were worked by slaves and gave Athens the constant advantage of a wealth which was greater than that of almost every other city in Greece.

The first victories for the people

During the Mycenaean epoch, Athens was governed by a king. About 700 B.C. the king was overthrown by his nobles and they assumed the government of the city. They attempted to impose the power of their rule arbitrarily: there were in fact no written laws in existence at that time and they governed from moment to moment according to the dictates of tradition and 'good sense', which often coincided with their personal interests. The Athenian people's first great victory, then, was the obtaining of written law before which it was impossible to equivocate. These laws were drawn up by Dracon in 621 B.C. and his written laws were so severe that even today the adjective 'draconian' implies great harshness.

Solon's reforms

As Athens grew annually more prosperous, the merchants and the artisans who made it so began to acquire huge fortunes. Despite being made free citizens and despite faithfully serving the polis (the city state) in peace and in war, the common people possessed absolutely no political power. Their wish to change things was shared by the small rural proprietors, by former farmers who had been ruined by debt and by the proud and honest citizens. In the city, conflict between these groups and the nobles reached such a stage that it became necessary to entrust the responsibility for political reform to a man famous for his fine sense of justice and who was an expert in government. That man was Solon. In 594 B.C. he brought to fruition a bill of reform which divided Athenian society, according to wealth, into five different classes. The richest citizens were pressed into military service in the cavalry and were personally required to pay the high costs of the equipment. In return they were eligible for election to any public office. The poorer citizens were recruited at the city's expense into the ranks of the light infantry or the navy. They were not permitted to be elected to public office, but did have the right to participate in the 'ecclesia', which was the most important of all the public assemblies, and they had the right to vote in the election of the magistrates.

Democracy for every citizen

The years which followed Solon's reforms, however, were often extremely turbulent and the battle between the great merchants, the large landowners, the peasants and the more humble artisans was fought furiously.

Finally, a new reform, brought about by Clistenes, brought a truly comprehensive and democratic system of government to the polis. Every citizen was granted membership of the Assembly, the supreme organ of the polis. Every citizen became eligible for all public offices. A 'bule' – a council of 500 members who were chosen annually by the drawing of lots – directed the work of the Assembly, which always retained sovereign power.

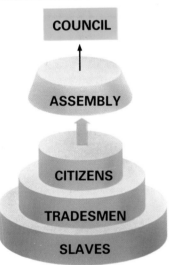

Reconstruction of a typical city in Ancient Greece. In the foreground we can see the agora in which commercial activities were conducted and public assemblies held. In the background we can see some of the city's more important buildings: the temple, the theatre and the sports ground.

lived in Athens for generations; anyone who was not an Athenian of 'pure blood' was denied the right to participate in the governing of his home city.

Further, 80,000 slaves (an average of two for every 'true' Athenian citizen) – were also excluded. We must think of them, and their sometimes very sad plight, when we consider the marvels of Athens and her citizens.

Athenian democracy survived personal ambitions and party rivalries with remarkably little in the way of disturbances. The most violent single act was the assassination of one of the leaders who had dared to attempt to strip the assembly of its power.

The limits of Athenian democracy

One obvious fact catches one's immediate attention on looking at the illustration above, and that is that Athenian democracy was a privilege reserved for few. Out of about 250,000 people (the estimated population of the city for this period), only about 40,000 in fact directly participated in it.

Excluded from taking part in this democracy were women and the younger children of true, fully-fledged Athenian citizens. Also excluded were the so-called 'Meteci' (meaning 'those who live around') as the foreign residents of Athens were named.

It did not matter that one's family had

OSTRACISM

The fear that one man – even if simply because of his widespread popularity – would attempt to set himself up as a 'tyrant', persuaded the Athenians to invent an original defence against the possibility: ostracism.

The person suspected would be tried before the Assembly and each citizen could inscribe the name of the dangerous personage on a piece of earthenware, which is called 'ostrakon' in Greek and of which we can see two examples on the right. It took the votes of only 6,000 citizens to ensure that the person concerned was exiled for the public good (without loss of honour or possessions) for as many as ten years.

ATHENS AGAINST SPARTA

In a history littered with inter-city rivalries, of contests between one polis and another, the years of the great war between the Persian Empire and the Greek world can be seen as a time of unity. Afterwards, the rival city states recommenced their struggle with a vengeance. Greece itself was altered as a result. We must also not forget, however, that even as the city-states warred amongst themselves they were continuing to develop the new and more profound elements of unity. Today, Sparta is no more than a heap of ruins, whilst Athens stands as a great monument to her own past. These monuments remain, despite the wars, as a more potent reminder of the spirit of Ancient Greece.

The triumph of Athens

At Marathon, Salamis, Plataea, Cape Mycale, all battles won by Greece, the Greek flea managed to confound the Persian elephant! In other words, the Greek army routed invading Persian troops.

Athens above all benefited from these victories. She gathered about herself a very powerful league of allies and gained dominance over something in the region of 300 wealthy cities. With the taxes collected from the allied states and dispensed by the magistrates, Athens was rebuilt and filled with splendid monuments.

Leading the city at the time was a man of noble birth, endowed with genuine democratic sentiments: Pericles.

He was re-elected to power for more than thirty years, from 461 to 429 B.C. This was the period of Athens's greatest splendour and became known as the 'Era of Pericles'.

The city rebuilt the Acropolis, which had been devastated by the Persians, and enriched itself with notable monuments. It filled up with artists, scientists, great playwrights and scholars. From the port of Piraeus sailed more than 300 warships, each with three banks of oars. These were the triremes, masters of the Mediterranean. Hundreds of trading vessels conducted business with the innumerable allied states, with the conquered, or with the colonies scattered from Spain to Africa and to the Black Sea.

The war between Sparta and Athens

The hard, brave and aristocratic city of Sparta represented one centre of Greece; the sophisticated, dynamic and democratic city of Athens, another. There was, almost inevitably, always conflict between the two great leading cities.

Between Athens and Sparta there began a war (which was, incidentally, fuelled directly by the Persians who supported Sparta) that even involved most of Greece's overseas colonies for almost thirty years.

Between 431 and 404 B.C. they fought everywhere. The war finished with the defeat of Athens which preserved its artistic and cultural leadership but was deprived of effective political weight.

Sparta, however, did not quite manage to dominate the peninsula. Surprisingly, standing against her still was the city of Thebes.

For a week once in every four years, everything in Greece came to a halt, even the wars that were being fought. This was to celebrate the 'Olympiad', religious ceremonies which were held in Olympia, the 'sacred city', in honour of Zeus, the greatest of gods. The Olympics comprised running, jumping, discus throwing and javelin competitions, as well as boxing and chariot-racing. The winners received only a symbolic prize, a crown of leaves taken from the enormous olive tree which grew in front of the temple of Zeus and they were honoured more than if they had won a battle.

The Olympic games were held from 776 B.C. until A.D. 393, an incredible 1,169 years. They were seen as so important by the Greeks that they measured their calendar from 776 B.C.

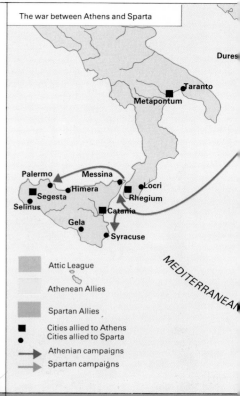

The war between Athens and Sparta

Dures

Taranto
Metapontum

Palermo — Messina
Segesta — Himera
Selinus — Locri
Rhegium
Catania
Gela
Syracuse

MEDITERRANEAN

Attic League

Athenean Allies

Spartan Allies

■ Cities allied to Athens
● Cities allied to Sparta
→ Athenian campaigns
→ Spartan campaigns

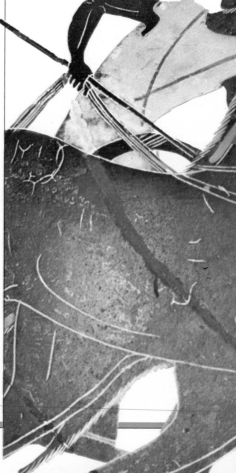

Right: Unlike modern atheletes, Greek runners did not run against each other wearing the minimum of clothing, but often wore heavy military clothing – some athletes were even handicapped by having to carry shields.

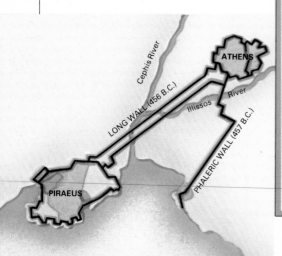

Cephis River
ATHENS
LONG WALL (456 B.C.)
Illissos River
PHALERIC WALL (457 B.C.)
PIRAEUS

The Spartans are defeated

In July of 371 B.C. for the first time ever, a Spartan army was defeated in open battle. What is more, only 6,000 Theban infantry defeated 10,000 Spartan foot soldiers. The Theban general, Epaminondas, achieved this victory – which ended the supremacy of Sparta in Greece – by deploying his troops in a novel fashion. In place of the 'normal' deployment, he arranged his ranks in such a way that the left wing was more advanced than the centre and the right wing. The Spartans violently attacked the weakest point, the centre. They encountered very little resistance, however, because the Theban centre purposely retreated. Simultaneously, the left wing carried out – almost as if they were drawing the shape of a wheel – a circular manoeuvre, which completely surrounded the enemy and left them with no escape route.

This tactic became famous throughout the Mediterranean and was copied by other generals in less important battles. Even today, the tactic is still studied by officer-cadets at military colleges all over the world.

Below: Chariot-races were the events with which the Olympic games were opened. On the right, the head of a youth, seen wearing a band probably designed to support the garland of olive-leaves which was awarded to the victor in each event.

ZEUS: THE GREATEST OF ALL

Even if they did fight amongst themselves, all the Greeks worshipped the same deities. Zeus was the most important, the incarnation of the heavens, of the lightning and of the thunder; Ge, of the earth, and Poseidon, god of the sea, Ares, god of war, and so on. Originally represented in human form, they were brought offerings of humans, animals and precious possessions. With the passing of time, the divinities became representative of more abstract ideas. Athene stood for courage and intelligence, Aphrodite symbolised beauty and love and Dionysius the ancient agrarian myth of the god who is born and dies every year like the vegetation.

The Greeks in the Mediterranean

To depart was painful for the old and amusing for the young. The old thought: 'How sad to leave the fatherland, the countryside, the feasts in honour of the dead, and the work of a whole lifetime.' But they had to leave. There was no more space at home for them to develop and expand, and to bring up their families as they had been brought up.

So they celebrated the old, eternal rites. They took a piece of earth and kissed it, knowing it would be reborn in foreign lands. They took an olive branch from their home, a divine symbol, knowing that it would grow on foreign soil and that it would protect them wherever they went. As well as a divine symbol, the olive tree was also important, as it gave shelter from the sun, wood to burn and oil for cooking and for lamps.

The youngsters only admired the splendid triremes waiting in the port, and were anxious to 'gallop' over the sea. What sea could be foreign to a Greek? What land was so far off that it could not be tamed?

Eventually, the swift triremes hoisted the mast with the sails and the captain called to them to embark. Half the city departed in this way, taken wherever there was land waiting for them to settle, these people in search of a new homeland.

A 6th century B.C. Spartan cup, with a commercial scene showing several merchants weighing their payments in the warehouse.

The trireme was a warship which was also used as a merchant vessel. It was characterised by its lightness and shallow draught (the part of the hull that remains immersed in the water) which enabled it to be beached every evening. They were of long, sleek shape (around 35–40 metres by 6 metres) which allowed them to sail at speeds of up to 5 knots (1 knot = 1,852 metres per hour) and were highly manoeuvrable. The crew consisted of about 200 men: the captain, ten officers, two archers, 14 infantrymen and 170 oarsmen. It is calculated that the weight of the trireme, including the crew, was 50 tons plus another 50 tons of ballast for optimum stability.

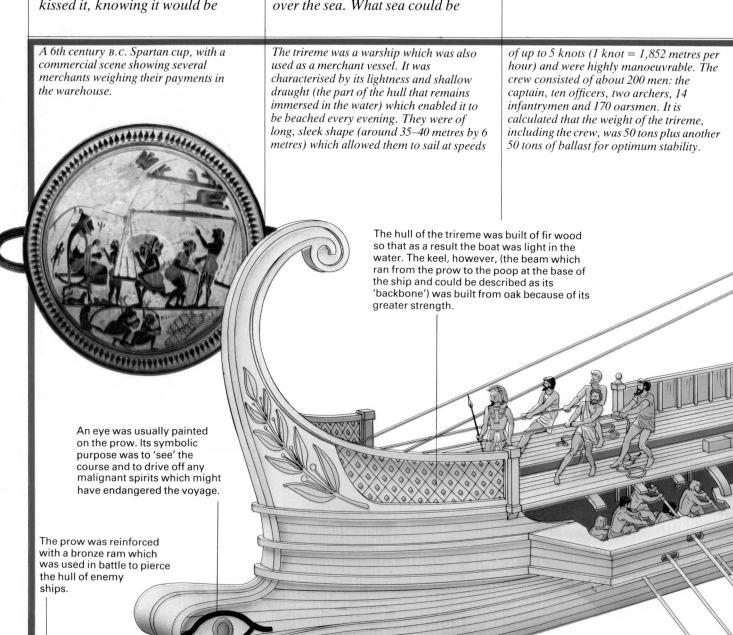

The hull of the trireme was built of fir wood so that as a result the boat was light in the water. The keel, however, (the beam which ran from the prow to the poop at the base of the ship and could be described as its 'backbone') was built from oak because of its greater strength.

An eye was usually painted on the prow. Its symbolic purpose was to 'see' the course and to drive off any malignant spirits which might have endangered the voyage.

The prow was reinforced with a bronze ram which was used in battle to pierce the hull of enemy ships.

NOT COLONIES, BUT INDEPENDENT CITY STATES

The word 'colony', which we use today, does not mean exactly the same as the Greek 'colonisation'. Although it may seem that the Greek citizens fled, that they were in competition with the city of their birth and that they left with the simple intention of defeating and dominating the natives that they encountered, this is not the case at all. Any departure to found new colonies was something deeply considered by the families involved, as well as by the State which valued highly the political benefits of setting up new colonies in certain areas. What would the king who ruled this territory do? Were they risking international complications? War, perhaps? Thus, the setting up of a normal colony was a voluntary

'apoikia', a term which is difficult to translate but which means both 'emigration' and 'the leaving of an inhabited place'.

The polis was generally in favour of this type of emigration; over-population and homelessness were two of the major problems it faced. It provided the ships, the livestock, the seeds and the equipment that the emigrants would need. But once the new colonists had disembarked and were sufficiently organised, the triremes sailed away. The colony was now an independent city-state. But the language, the clothing, the traditions and the culture were all the same as the mother city's. Fundamentally the Greeks understood that these basic links were much more important than a relationship based on the political domination of a subservient people.

THE FABULOUS TRIREME 15

The vessel we see illustrated in the diagram below was the basis on which Greece in general, and Athens in particular, founded their fortunes. The ship was called a trireme simply because of the three banks of oars on each side. The diagram below shows how all three were situated. Strong, but at the same time fast and manageable, it was for centuries the mistress of the Mediterranean.

Usually described as a warship, it could be said that the trireme was the 'queen' of the many battles she fought.

But it was also the rapid vehicle used to transport thousands of Greeks overseas to colonise new lands and to maintain contact between the colonies and the motherland.

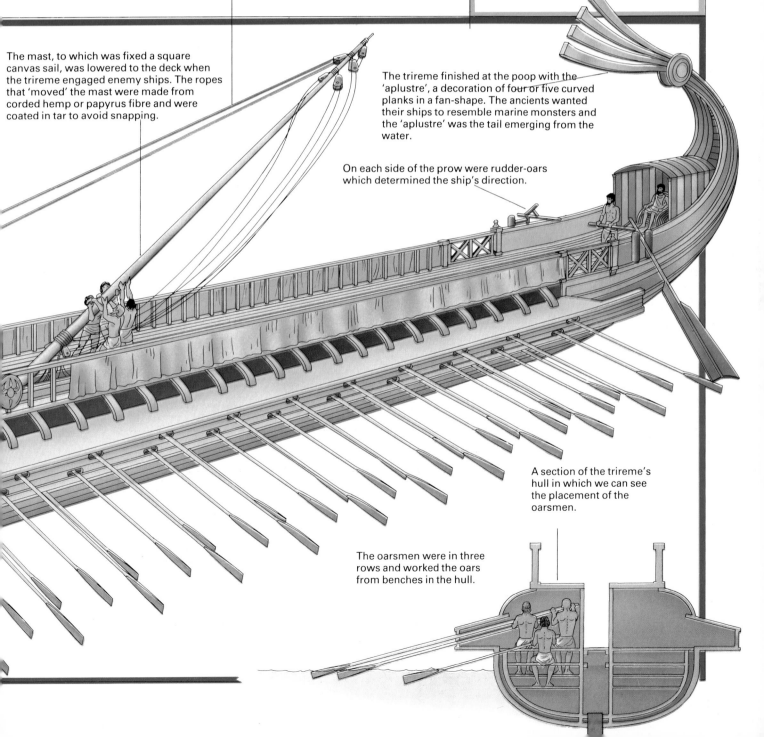

The mast, to which was fixed a square canvas sail, was lowered to the deck when the trireme engaged enemy ships. The ropes that 'moved' the mast were made from corded hemp or papyrus fibre and were coated in tar to avoid snapping.

The trireme finished at the poop with the 'aplustre', a decoration of four or five curved planks in a fan-shape. The ancients wanted their ships to resemble marine monsters and the 'aplustre' was the tail emerging from the water.

On each side of the prow were rudder-oars which determined the ship's direction.

A section of the trireme's hull in which we can see the placement of the oarsmen.

The oarsmen were in three rows and worked the oars from benches in the hull.

FROM GIBRALTAR TO THE BLACK SEA

The first phase of Greek colonisation can be traced back to the Mycenaean era (around 1400 B.C.). The conquest of Crete and the other islands in the Aegean represented the first movement of expansion. The war for Troy, even, could be considered a colonial war, on which depended the survival of the Achaean holdings in the lands and waters of the Eastern Mediterranean.

Subsequent powerful expeditions took place between the eighth and sixth centuries B.C. During this period many hundreds of Greek colonists left their homeland in search of fortune along the western coasts of the Mediterranean. In Greece it was not easy to find work and wealth: the cities were overpopulated and the fertile land was in the hands of a few owners.

The map below shows the parts of the Mediterranean that were colonised by the Greeks and what these colonies provided.

The 'Greece of Asia'

The first flux of Greek colonists went to the coasts of Asia Minor because this was the nearest land and the easiest to reach via the Aegean islands.

All along the western coast of Asia Minor dozens of new Greek cities sprang up. There were three main regions: Aeolis, Ionia and Dorica, corresponding to the three principal Greek peoples – the Aeolians, the Ionians and the Dorians.

The cities founded in Asia Minor were considered equal to the cities of Greece itself and they became completely autonomous and just as commercially wealthy. It was for this very reason that the Greek cities in Asia Minor constituted what was called 'Asian Greece' which means that even in this area we can discover every characteristic of the civilisation of Ancient Greece.

A perfect example of Greek civilisation in Asia was the city of Miletus in Ionia. In the seventh century before Christ the Greeks pushed as far as the Black Sea which they called Pontus Euxinus, meaning 'the hospitable sea'.

Wherever they went, the Greeks took with them their traditions, religions and their theatre; and they built beautiful buildings in their classic styles – Doric, Corinthian and Ionic.

'GREAT GREECE'

The greatest amount of Greek colonisation took place along the coasts of the Mediterranean. The interest of the Greek colonists turned towards Sicily and southern Italy. Thus many colonies were founded which were given the name 'Great Greece' because they possessed in equal measure all the qualities which characterised Greece herself. Fertile lands, plains ideal for grazing, perfect secure ports and a gentle climate.

In the Mediterranean the Greeks had to confront other nations involved in the intense commercial trade taking place. The most aggressive amongst these were the Phoenicians. The Phoenicians had also established numerous colonies, amongst which was Qart-Hadasht (which means 'new city') on the coast of Africa, and which the Ancient Romans were later to call Carthage.

The Greeks also pushed as far as Africa. There they founded Cyrenia in a fertile region, rich in fruit trees, wheat and pasture land. Other rich and important Greek colonies were Marsiglia (Marseilles) in France and Saguntum in Spain. To the east of Marsiglia, the Greeks founded other colonies on the sites of Nice, Monaco and Antibes.

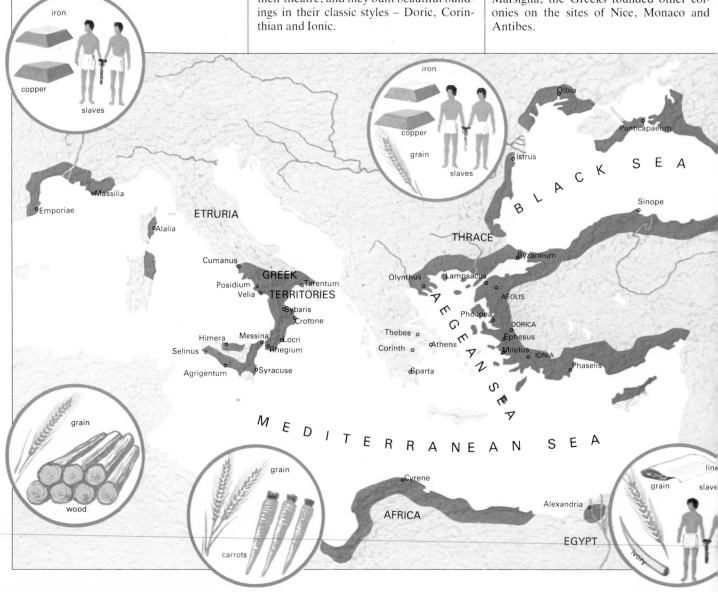

THE MEDITERRANEAN – A GREEK LAKE?

This is a very natural question if you look at the map on the previous page. It shows the spread of Greek civilisation from Gibraltar to the Black Sea, from Spain to the north of Africa. All along the Mediterranean coastline there were cities founded by Greeks who had left their homeland bringing their own ideas of civilisation with them. Unlike the Persian Empire of a few centuries earlier, which was aiming to conquer the world and impose Persian rule on it, the Greeks co-existed happily with the peoples who lived around their cities.

THE GREEK LEGACY

Had the Greeks never left their homeland we would possibly know little about their way of life at this time, other than through myths and stories handed down from generation to generation.

But because the Greeks did take to their elegant triremes and colonise the Mediterranean, they left behind a legacy that still influences us today.

Their architecture, their political beliefs and their ideal of democracy are all part of our common heritage and we are all, even in the twentieth century, indebted to them in some way or another.

An aerial view of Cyrene, an exceptionally rich Greek colony, founded in 630 B.C. on the coast of northern Africa. It was blessed with a fertile soil and produced an abundance of grain, oil, fruit and precious spices which the Greeks used to flavour their food, and for medical purposes as well. Archaeological digs around Cyrene have been of immense value and have shown that during its heyday, Cyrene must have been one of the richest towns in the Greek Empire. Numerous pieces of pottery have been found that show that the Cyrenean citizens had a particularly strong relationship (both trading and cultural) with the citizens of Athens.

A view of Paestum, or Posidonia, a Greek colony founded in the seventh century B.C. in southern Italy. The Greeks referred to the colony as Posidonia; Paestum is the Roman name which was given to it in the third century B.C. The colony flourished thanks to the development of its trading links with other Greek colonies along the Tyrrhenian Sea. It reached its height in the fifth century B.C. This was when the temples shown here were built. They were designed on a grand scale and are still, today, in a very good state of preservation. The most famous temple in Paestum is the Temple to Poseidon (right in the photograph). A tomb has been found and, even now, more than two thousand years after the tomb was built, much of its decorative work maintains amazing freshness of colour and can be seen in the nearby museum.

The Greatest Greek

In the north of Greece during the fourth century B.C. a new power arose. The area of Macedon was large and populous, but so backward that most Greeks were reluctant to acknowledge any sort of kinship with the people who lived there. The Macedonians were hardened by wars against many non-Greek peoples.

In 359 B.C. Philip the Second inherited the throne of Macedon. He disposed of his rivals with ruthless efficiency and paid off his barbarian neighbours, to ensure permanent peace.

He then turned his attention to the problem of divided Greece. At a time when citizens of most Greek states were beginning to prefer to hire mercenary soldiers to fight for them if the need arose, Philip commanded a hardened and disciplined band of trained soldiers. After twenty years of intermittent war, Philip controlled most of northern Greece. Then Athens and Thebes formed an alliance to resist him, but Philip defeated them at the battle of Chaeronea in 338 B.C. and the age of the city states came to an end. Thebes and other cities were garrisoned by Macedonian troops and Athens made a separate peace, although she and the other Greek states had to join a new confederation organised by Philip, with himself as the 'elected' head. The aim of this 'Corinthian League' was to march against their common Persian enemy.

Philip was on the point of doing so when he was stabbed while taking part in a procession. No one knows who was responsible. It may have been the Persians, or his wife, Olympias, or even the man who was to succeed him – his son Alexander, whom we now know as Alexander the Great.

A TWENTY-YEAR-OLD GENIUS

Alexander was just twenty years of age when he inherited the throne. The Greek city states which Philip had forced to join the Corinthian League were not saddened by his death. Alexander marched into their midst and forced them to elect him leader. He possessed the ability to move swiftly – more swiftly than his opponents believed possible. He was quite ruthless and, perhaps most important of all, he was completely dedicated to his own glory. As an example of his ruthlessness, when he was away campaigning, the people of Thebes broke out in revolt against the Macedonian garrison. Alexander returned to Greece, stormed the city, sold its inhabitants into slavery and razed the city to the ground.

Then, still only 22, he crossed into Asia to march against the Persians.

He crossed the Hellespont with 40,000 men and immediately met a Persian army which he routed at the battle of Granicus in 334 B.C. This freed Asiatic Greece from Persian rule. His enemies expected him to march on into western Asia, but, instead, he marched into Syria, attempting to cut the Persians off from the Mediterranean. The Persian king, Darius, tried to stop him, but chose as a battleground land that was such that his superiority in numbers could not be made effective, and Alexander beat him so thoroughly that he was able to capture Darius's wife and daughters.

Alexander refused Darius's offer of peace and went on to occupy Phoenicia and Palestine. He besieged the great port of Tyre – a siege that lasted for seven months, during which time the Spartans revolted and the Persians counter-attacked in Asia Minor.

Alexander coped with both the rebellion and the counter-attack and eventually stormed and destroyed Tyre. He marched on into Egypt where he founded the city that bore his name – Alexandria. While in Egypt he was hailed as a new pharaoh and the son of the god Ammon. It is quite possible that Alexander believed himself to be a god, too.

In 331 B.C. Alexander crossed the Euphrates and the Tigris and at Gaugamela faced a huge Persian army headed by Darius. The Greek out-manoeuvred his enemy and Darius fled, to be murdered by his own men.

Alexander marched from Babylon into Persia, itself, capturing the cities of Susa, Persepolis and Ecbatana. At Persepolis Alexander captured the enormous gold reserves of the Persians and then burned the royal palace to commemorate his victory.

He had still not finished. The huge, mountainous areas of East Persia still refused to bow to him and it took him three more years to bend them to his will. Eventually the whole of Persia was under his control, but he was still not satisfied. He marched on and overran the Punjab. It seemed that he would indeed master the world, but his troops became weary of fighting and refused to go on. It is said that they were intimidated by the Indian war-elephants, but whatever the reason, in 325 B.C. Alexander was forced to turn back.

When he arrived back in Babylon he found that many of the governors whom he had appointed to rule in his absence had believed that they would never see him again and had assumed too much power. Alexander dealt with them ruthlessly.

He then decided to attempt to fuse Macedonia, Greece and Persia into a single country. He arranged for 30,000 young Persians to begin military training under Macedonian instructors. He appointed Persians as well as Macedonians to govern his provinces while he was away campaigning and he assumed the title of Great King.

Alexander's followers failed to understand his lenient behaviour towards the Persians. It was quite alien to the Greek way and they were also alienated by his semi-divine monarchical style – also very un-Greek.

Despite plots against him which he dealt with with ruthlessness, Alexander kept the loyalty of his army, partly because of the way he shared the hardships and dangers of campaign life with his men. But once he returned to Persia, after his Indian war, the army turned against his plan to mix Persian and Macedonian soldiers within its ranks.

Alexander, however, persuaded his army to obey him after he threatened to dismiss them all.

He then encouraged the Macedonian soldiers to marry Persian girls. Thousands of them did, including Alexander. He married Darius's daughter. East, he claimed, had married West. His aim was to create a master race larger than the Greeks themselves could provide, to control all the non-Greek, Macedonian and Persian peoples in his empire.

He also believed that the Greeks and Persians would work together more harmoniously if united in the worship of a god-king – himself.

He seems to have secured the Greeks' acceptance of his god-status in 324 B.C. but died the following year – aged only 33. Some say that he died of fever, others that he died from over-eating and over-drinking. Whatever the cause of his death, and the eventual crumbling of his Empire – there is little doubt that Alexander deserved (and still deserves) the 'Great' that we add to his name.

Alexander had believed himself to be immortal and had carelessly made no arrangements for the government of his empire after he died. Almost as soon as he died, his empire, held together mainly by his power and personality, began to fall apart. His generals scrambled for power and many of them set themselves up as kings in the fragments of the empire where they held power. Two of them founded dynasties that were named after them – Ptolomy in Egypt and Seleucus in western Asia.

Although Alexander's dream of an ever-lasting Greco-Persian empire failed to materialise, the lands that he conquered remained Greek, culturally speaking. The Ptolomies remained a Greek dynasty and were great patrons of Greek artists and scholars, and in Asia, even after the Indian and Iranian areas of Alexander's empire won their independence, they continued to use Greek coins and speak the Greek language.

The Greek Genius

The men of the first great civilisation studied nature and the movement of the stars, they discovered mathematical rules and created works of great art, all with a practical purpose. In Greece, for the first time ever, questions were asked such as, 'What is the world?' 'What sense is there to life?' We understand immediately that the answers to these questions have changed throughout the centuries but Greek research gave birth to almost all the fundamental modern sciences. This, then, was the triumph of the intelligence, of the 'genius' of Ancient Greece.

A statue from the fifth century B.C. showing Athene in thought. The goddess, who was born fully armed from the head of Zeus, was the inspiration for great acts of war and battle strategies. She symbolised the supremacy of the intellect and courage over force. She was the protector of women, marriage and children as well as the symbol of intelligence, reason and spirit. Athene was considered to be the inspirer and inventor of all instruments used in the developments of arts, sciences and crafts.

SCIENTIFIC REASONING

Not all of the theories formulated by the ancient philosopher-scientists are reasonable. Some of them are simply unsophisticated, whilst others are very obviously wrong. On the other hand, some of them come surprisingly close to what we today have 're-discovered' and substantiated with very different instruments of research. One splendid example of this is that 2,400 years ago the Greek philosopher Democritus guessed that the structure fundamental to all matter was atomic: this was only confirmed by modern science – albeit using very different methods – at the beginning of this century. Furthermore, over and above the many basic errors, there was a further benefit gained: for the first time ever, the Greek 'philosopher-scientists' applied what we today would describe as 'logic' and 'a scientific method'. This was a tremendous advance for humanity which for thousands of years had accepted 'magical' explanations for natural phenomena.

Earth and the Universe

Observation and scientific reasoning allowed Aristarchus of Samos (c. 310–230 B.C.), even in the absence of today's perfect instrumentation, to understand and describe the 'mechanism' of the solar system. He deduced that the Sun, many times larger than the Earth, was the star around

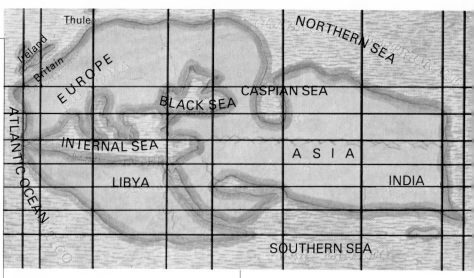

which the other planets, including Earth, rotated.

Geography, the description of the surface of the Earth, took several notable steps forward in more or less the same period.

In the illustration above we see the geographical map designed by Eratosthenes in 200 B.C. It becomes even more remarkable when we remember the almost negligible means of surveying then at his disposal.

Why was technical development so limited?

The Greeks were extremely advanced in terms of understanding physical and mechanical phenomena: the deductions and practical conclusions drawn by Heron of Alexandria were a direct anticipation of those drawn in the nineteenth century (steam machines) and twentieth century (principle of reaction). Yet these brilliant discoveries were applied only to making playthings or for 'curiosity' value – destined more to amaze and delight rather than ever be truly utilised. Why were they not applied in a large-scale industrial way which would certainly have accelerated the progress of the entire Greek world?

There are two answers to this question. The first is technological: the technical means then at their disposal would not have permitted the construction of these machines. The second answer concerns the

banks of seats
orchestra entrance
orchestra
altar
stage
seats for high-priests and magistrates

The theatrical season in Greece lasted ten days each year. For this period, the Greeks made their way to the theatre in the woods and spent the whole day there, taking food along to eat during the intervals. To the poorer spectators, the state reimbursed the price of a ticket. The actors, made more impressive by masks and elevated footwear, recited three tragedies and a satire, or five comedies, every day.

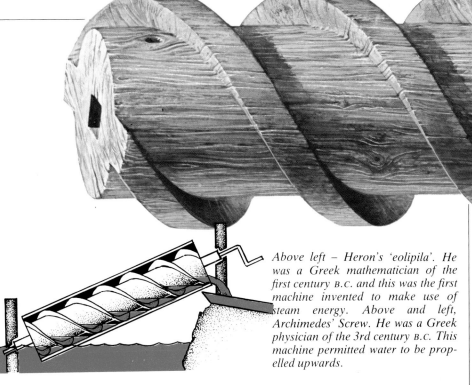

social order of the time; there was little need to invent machines to relieve man's workload since slaves were readily available for precisely that purpose.

Thought rules the world

'In a right-angled triangle, the square on the hypotenuse is equal to the sum of the squares on the other two sides.' This, the famous theorem of the great Pythagoras, is a piece of pure, logical reasoning. Of course, Pythagoras' theorem is useful in a practical sense, but what really counts is the discovery of the mathematical principle.

In geometry, we can honestly say that nothing has changed since Euclid's day. He

was another brilliant Greek mathematician. A few things have been added and perfected, but the basis of our geometrical knowledge is still the Greek or Euclidean (the two are considered the same) system and this is illustrated by the fact that many of the terms we use are Greek. In our own

Above left – Heron's 'eolipila'. He was a Greek mathematician of the first century B.C. and this was the first machine invented to make use of steam energy. Above and left, Archimedes' Screw. He was a Greek physician of the 3rd century B.C. This machine permitted water to be propelled upwards.

very recent times some scientists have proposed a new form of geometry but in our schools we are still using the system formulated by the Ancient Greeks. The new theory is not designed to show any error in Euclid's system, it simply attempts to show a new means of examining the world from a geometric point of view, without detracting in the slightest from the ancient system.

TECHNIQUE AND ART

To Ancient Greece we owe the invention of one of the greatest forms of artistic expression: the theatre. The works of great tragic authors, such as Aeschylus, Sophocles and Euripides, and brilliant comic authors such as Aristophanes, are still performed in theatres all over the world today .

For the Greeks, however, theatre was more of a ritual than an entertainment. For this reason, it was a point of honour for every polis to build a theatre, testifying to its importance. Here, science came to the aid of art; the theatres, normally in the open air, were semi-circular in shape and were often on a small hill. This helped support the banks of seats (the 'cavea'), where the spectators took their places. At the base of this, on the other hand, was the 'orchestra', an open semi-circular space where the

chorus stood or the dances were performed, while the 'scena', the actual stage itself, was more to the rear in an elevated position, in such a way that everyone could see the actors (who were exclusively male). Despite their size, the acoustics in these attractive buildings were perfect. From high up in the very back row one heard every whisper by an actor on the stage.

Because they had to be seen and understood from almost one hundred metres away, and from many different angles, Greek actors used masks and strongly patterned costumes, and acted with formalised gestures. Such conventions made intimate effects impossible and Greek drama never broke away from its ritual origins.

Every nation in history has created works of art that we deem masterpieces. But the Greeks, sought – successfully – to express that which is beautiful, simply because of its beauty. Thus, Greek poetry did not have practical ends; it was not a prayer or an invocation to the gods, but had the sole purpose of bringing us to an understanding of the harmony and beauty hidden in things which the words of the poet sought to reveal.

Also in Greek sculpture, the artist was not satisfied merely to represent the human form realistically, but instead to put all his efforts into rendering that beauty, that sense of harmony, which is present in the world of living forms.

Pythagoras was the first person to realise that a relationship existed between the tone and the length of a musical cord. In the diagram below we see a musical string divided into equal parts and slowly shortened from 11 to 9, 9 to 7, and 7 to 5. By moving down the cord, each note became higher in tone.

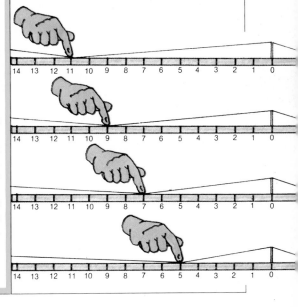

In the world today, there are perhaps six cities called Athens and a couple of dozen called Rome. They are usually small-sized towns or simple villages, and so it is impossible to calculate exactly how many there are. However it is interesting to observe that most of them are found in the Americas and in Australia, lands which Europeans colonised in recent centuries. It is as if, searching for a new existence over the ocean, the children of the Old World wanted to take with them a memory of their history, the richness of an inimitable past. In fact, the names of these two cities sum up human progress in the ancient world, a heritage which is the foundation of our civilisation. Rome grew from a federation of villages to the centre of one of the longest-lasting empires the world has seen . . .

21st APRIL 753 B.C.

According to tradition it was on the 21st April in the year 753 B.C. that Rome was born. This was the feast of the goddess Pales, the protector of the herds. To celebrate this feast all the shepherds belonging to the people of the Latins gathered from the hills and the valleys along the river Tiber. It was a feast that had been repeated for decades. However, this time it was a memorable occasion. The height of the ceremony was to be the foundation of a new city, the name of which had already been chosen: Rome.

Some people maintain that Rome comes from the name of Etruscan origin: the noble family of Ruma or Rumla (which became Romulus) which underlines the Etruscan influence in the birth of the city on the Tiber.

Others maintain that – and this is the most credible version – the name derives from the Etruscan Rumon – river, or from the root of the verb to flow, ru. So Rome would be the 'city on the river', and from here came the name of its king Rumulus or Romulus, the 'Lord of the River'.

A favourable position

The initiative was taken by those of the tribe of Ramnes, 'the river people'. However, a part was played by the families of the tribe of Tities, shepherds belonging to the Sabine people who lived a few miles away.

Shepherds in that area had been scraping an existence for centuries. However, the Etruscans, the Lucani, the Greeks and even the Phoenicians who came by ship grew rich in this place. In fact, from the nearby Tyrrennian Sea (less than 24 kilometres away) they went up the river with their merchandise and met the merchants who came down from inside Latium and those who travelled from North to South and vice versa, passing below the Palatine hill and crossing the river at the natural ford at the island in the middle of the Tiber.

A fortified city built on this steep Palatine hill would be able to control all this lucrative trade. This was the idea of the Ramnes people: a city where they could defend themselves and at the same time flourish.

The birth of the new city

The ceremonies had begun. They were led

The Birth of Rome

by the chief of the Ramnes. They called him Romulus: maybe it was a nickname or maybe it was a title meaning Lord of the River. From Etruria came the priests, musicians, fortune tellers and soothsayers who foretold the future by observing the flight of birds and the entrails of sacrificed animals – they were well paid. The prophecies were excellent: it seemed that Rome was to enjoy the particular favour of the gods.

According to ancient custom, perfected by the Etruscans, Romulus traced a line round the perimeter where the walls were to be raised. A mighty bull was tied to a plough on the outside; a strong young heifer was placed on the inside. There was a reason for this: the strength of the bull would fall upon the enemies who tried to attack the walls from outside; the fertility of the heifer was to be an example to the women of the city of Rome who were to fill it up with sons. Romulus stopped the plough at the place corresponding to the future gate in the wall and inside it the land was not to be touched. Only friends and allies could pass within.

Meanwhile on the altar, great sacrifices were being made: a black ram, a pig and a

A map of the peoples which inhabited the Italian peninsula at the time of the founding of Rome.

bull. Their bodies were not to be totally burned, but buried along the ditch which indicated the future walls. In this way the wound inflicted on Mother Earth, with the plough, was placated and the strength of the three victims would be magically transferred to the city.

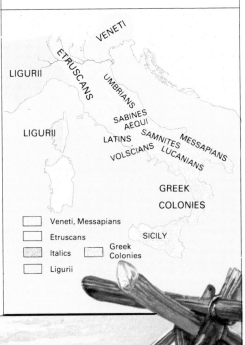

The legend of its origins

Still today the symbol of the city of Rome is the famous wolf suckling the twins Romulus and Remus. When they reached the height of their power the Romans recounted a legend to glorify the humble origins of their city.

The children of Mars, the god of war, and the legitimate heirs to the throne of the Latin city of Albalonga, the two newly-born babies Romulus and Remus, were abandoned in a basket and thrown into the Tiber on the orders of their wicked uncle who had usurped power. But the current of the river carried them to a bank where a she-wolf (or else the wife of a shepherd who was nicknamed 'Wolf') saved and raised them.

When they grew up and learned of their divine and regal origins, the two brothers immediately took vengeance. They decided to establish a new city but found themselves in disagreement over who was to be king.

Romulus traced out the ditch and as an act of disdain Remus jumped over it and his angry brother killed him.

This is how the legend goes.

Remus never existed

The Romans invented the legend of Romulus and Remus several centuries after the founding of the city, in the period when their monarchy had been abolished and they had to find a way of explaining how it came about that supreme power was in the hands of two magistrates, the consuls. This is proved by one fact: up until the end of the fourth century B.C. Roman tradition only remembered Romulus as the father of Rome. So what has a she-wolf got to do with it? Perhaps it was a sacred animal which the Ramnes, like all ancient tribes and peoples, had adopted as their protector and symbol. (The falcon of the pharaohs, the owl of Athens and the eagle of imperial Rome are other examples.)

Left. The foundation of Rome on the Palatine hill.
Below, bronze sculpture from the fifth or sixth century B.C. representing the she-wolf which suckled the twins Romulus and Remus.

HISTORY BEGAN LATE

History began late on the Italian peninsula. When the Egyptian pharaohs were building the pyramids, the Italian peoples were still living in caves. When the Cretans dominated the seas and the Achaeans conquered it, the most highly developed peoples on the peninsula had just discovered agriculture and were living in primitive villages built on planks over swamps. Rome was born in some obscurity, while in the east King Tiglath-pileser III was founding the mighty Syrian empire; at the same time in central Northern Italy, the Etruscan civilisation was spreading and in the south and in eastern Sicily the Greeks were beginning to set up colonies arriving from their native lands in the elegant triremes we read about on pages 14 and 15.

The peoples of Latium

In the heart of the Italian peninsula, around Latium, populations of farmers and shepherds had been living for centuries: real and proper Latins, Sabines, Aequines, Volsci, Samnites and Lucani to the south. . . . Every population was made up of various clans or tribes (large families): 300 to 400 people altogether, family groups and their servants and friends, gathered together in small areas (farms, fields and grazing lands). They were dominated by the absolute authority of the family chief who guided them in politics, war and religion. The main bond which united the tribe was that they spoke the same language, had the same habits and traditions and worshipped the same gods. This bond was particularly strong among the Latins, a more closely-knit community than the other tribes.

On fixed dates, these peoples gathered together at the city of Albalonga in the area of the temple of the greatest Latin god: Jupiter Latiaris, the king of the sky and the father of the gods, later identified with the Greek Zeus.

The various Latin tribes gathered together for religious ceremonies which then also became opportunities to strike up alliances, commercial relationships and defence treaties against common enemies. This sort of 'United States of Latium' in the ninth and eighth centuries B.C. was thrown into disorder with the founding of Rome.

The moderately important Latium states were probably dominated, or at least influenced by their Etruscan neighbours.

LATIUM AND ITS CITIES

In ancient times, Latium was made up of volcanic land which was fertile and favoured agriculture (cereals, legumes and other vegetables) and pasture (dairy produce, beef, pigs and sheep), and was densely populated and rich in cities as can be seen on the map below. On the left we can see the river Tiber and the layout of the seven hills on which Rome was built. Primitive Rome was more or less square-shaped; then the city grew and towards the middle of the sixth century B.C. under Servius Tullius, it was encircled by walls. During the Imperial era Rome grew and the Emperor Aurelius (A.D. 270–275) had it ringed by a new wall. During the Middle Ages, Rome shrank; only during the Renaissance did it develop again, influenced by the Roman Catholic church.

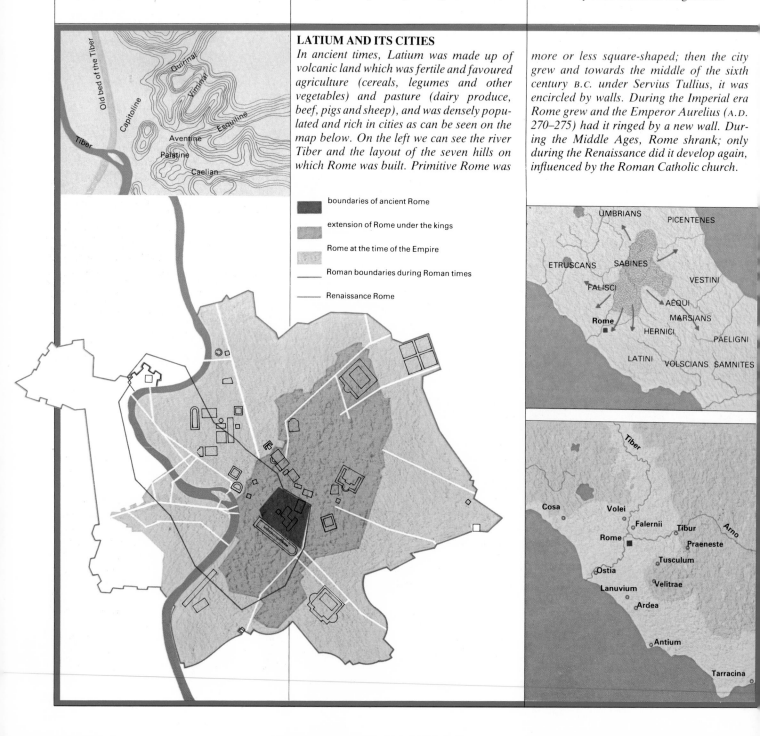

- boundaries of ancient Rome
- extension of Rome under the kings
- Rome at the time of the Empire
- Roman boundaries during Roman times
- Renaissance Rome

Latin and Sabine kings

We have seen the reasons for which the birth of a city like Rome was in a certain sense inevitable. We don't know if Romulus really traced out his ditch. However, we know that the Latin tribe of Ramnes, the neighbouring Sabine tribe of Tities (from their legendary chief Titus Tatius) and soon the Luceres were the original inhabitants of Rome, which was built on the Palatine hill and slowly spread to the surrounding hills. The Latin Ramnes were the main inhabitants of the Palatine hill; the Sabine Tities moved on to the Quirinal hill and the Luceres on to the Caelian (today the Lateran). The chiefs of the three tribes met on the plain between the Palatine and the Quirinal where the Forum, the real heart of Rome, was later to arise. Here they talked over affairs of common interest. It is not known exactly who the Luceres were: perhaps they were a conquered people or else lower ranking allies who were persuaded to join the new city. In the beginning however they were considered inferior, even if their chiefs took part in communal meetings.

This is also mentioned in the legendary tradition: the first four kings of Rome were alternately a Latin and a Sabine: Romulus, Numa Pompilius, Tullus Hostilius and Ancus Marcius.

Early organisation

The complicated origins of the city of Rome led the inhabitants of the city to set up a special type of organisation. It was divided into the three tribes of Ramnes, Tities and Luceres. Every tribe was divided into ten senate houses, and every senate house into ten peoples or families. This division was adopted mainly for military reasons. In fact every tribe had to provide 1,000 infantrymen and 100 horsemen to the army (one hundred infantrymen and ten horsemen for every family).

The real rulers of monarchic Rome were the powerful family chiefs.

They were all-powerful over their own people and in normal circumstances decided everything concerning their own group independently. However, out of common need, these 'fathers' (patres), these 'old men' (seniores, from which comes the title senator) elected a king.

He was basically a person equal to them and not a tyrant. He was invested with authority when he was chosen and confirmed by an assembly of all the senate houses together. These were the so-called Senate House Assemblies: guided by their clan chief, all the free citizens who gave military service voted for the acceptance or rejection of the king. The king had to call on the assembly of the 'fathers' – the senate – every time an important decision concerning the whole community had to be taken. As time passed, the exterior symbols of the

Early armour: above left, a breastplate, on the right, a leg guard, and alongside, a helmet.

king became more elaborate. The simple crown of oak leaves became a crown of gold; the shepherd's crook, an ivory sceptre tipped by the sacred animal of the god Jupiter. Like this god – of whom he was a representative and priest – he wore a mantle of purple and when he moved around he travelled in a gilded coach. But these were external signs. Real power rested with the assembly of the old family chiefs. The kings passed on, but the Senate remained.

Even at the outset, the kings seemed to have introduced the earliest of the civic amenities for which Rome was to become famous. The last king, Tarqinius Superbus, is said to have had built a system of public sewers.

Seven are too few

Ancient historians say that Roman monarchy lasted 244 years: from 753 B.C., the year of foundation, to 509 B.C. when the last king was expelled. There was a total of seven kings. If we consider this number, we will see that seven is not very many for such a long period. Each one would have had to have ruled for an average of 35 years. It is not impossible but it is improbable as the lifespan of men and women then was much shorter than it is today.

Today it seems certain that the names of the kings – at least the first four – were nothing but 'labels' used to indicate some important periods in the life of early Roman society.

THE END OF THE MONARCHY

The last three Roman kings were Etruscans: the Etruscan influence was the most important characteristic of the last ages of the Roman monarchy. Once again, legends help us to understand the complicated development of primitive Rome.

Lucumo in Rome

Roman writers explain the accession of the fifth Roman king with a surprising story.

The son of a rich foreign merchant (perhaps Greek) was married to an Etruscan noblewoman from the city of Tarquinia and had a son who was called Lucumo. Lucumo came to search for his fortune in Rome. With his skills he obtained the favour of the king Ancus Marcius who entrusted him with the education of his sons.

He grew rich and won the friendship of the tribe of Luceres, which up until then had been considered inferior to those of the Ramnes and the Tities. To win the favour of Rome he changed his name which was clearly Etruscan to a more Roman one: Lucius Tarquinius.

On the death of Ancus Marcius and without awaiting the decision of the patres, the austere senators, he called a meeting of the Senate House and with the support of the Luceres he was nominated king.

This support was immediately repaid; the family chiefs of the Luceres became part of the Senate. To the old 100–200 patres of ancient Ramnes or Sabine descent these conscriptea (additionals) were added to make up a fixed number of 300 senators who were nominated for life and equal to each other.

The Etruscans leave their mark

The legend probably hides an historical event. A powerful Etruscan clan took over Rome by exploiting the differences among the various tribes which ruled it. It is not

Below left, the outlet into the Tiber of the Cloaca Maxima; right, an earthenware head of an Etruscan god, the Hermes of Veii.

known exactly when this happened but it is a fact that the Luceres, who up until then were second-class citizens, grew rich and became more powerful until they entered the group of leaders which governed Rome. It is quite possible that they did this with the help of a 'strong man' who was half foreigner and whom they made king to break up the authority of the tribes which up until then had ruled Rome. However, what matters is the influence which the highly advanced Etruscan civilisation had on the development of Rome. Lucius Tarquinius called Priscus (the Old, the First) is known as one who made great improvements thanks to the superior technical abilities of the Etruscans. These included the draining of the swamps around the hills and the construction of a drainage system, the so-called Cloaca Maxima which – 25 centur-

ies later – is still partially in use. He introduced elements from Etruscan religious tradition, and built the Circus Maximus where shows, sports competitions and chariot races were held according to Etruscan tradition. The austere Latin tradition only survived in private life. Society was undergoing a rapid process of 'modernisation' through contact with the Etruscan civilisation which was considerably more advanced.

The expulsion of the kings

Under the sixth king, Servius Tullius, an Etruscan, Rome began to become 'great'. New walls surrounded the seven hills and the Latin cities recognised its supremacy. Servius Tullius's place was taken by another Etruscan king, who like those before him took power illegally: Tarquin the Proud (534–509 B.C.).

According to tradition he was the opposite of Servius Tullius. He was harsh, tyrannical, violent, greedy, and he upset the nobility and the Roman people alike. Popular reaction, skilfully guided by Roman nobility, forced the Etruscan king and his followers to abandon Rome. In the city which was now free of kings, a Republic was proclaimed and continued to exist for over five centuries.

Tarquin is best known to many of us as the man whom Shakespeare wrote about in *The Rape of Lucrece*, which event is supposed to have sparked off the revolt led by Junius Brutus which drove him from Rome. The word 'king' remained so odious to the Romans that five hundred years later, when the state was permanently ruled by one man, the Romans would not use the old word to describe him.

Home life

The pater of the great Roman family had the right of life and death over its members: relatives, hangers-on or servants – whatever they were. He was the law at home. He registered births and deaths: a new-born child only became part of the family after the public ceremony in which it was recognised by the father. If he accepted it as his son he held him on his knees. From that moment on it was a Roman citizen and among its many rights was that to a name. In fact it had the right to several names. It had a praenomen, a personal name like Lucius, Publius, Brutus or Caius. Then a nomen which indicated the 'people' he belonged to, such as Cornelius, a member of

the clan of the Cornelii, or Julius, of the clan of the Julii. But these clans contained more than one family group. So if necessary a third name, the cognomen, was added. The cognomen usually indicated the actual family he was born into, referring to some characteristic of an ancestor. So for example Marcus Tullius Cicero was: Marcus of the Tullius clan and the family whose ancestor had a verruca (cicero means verruca) on his face. In the same way Caius Julius Caesar was Caius of the famous Julian clan, belonging to the branch of those with bright eyes (one interpretation of 'Caesar').

. . . And outside the house

Roman society during the monarchical era

was essentially an agricultural society. The family chiefs and their clans usually lived outside the city. The city was usually left to the craftsmen, the merchants and the people who had no fixed job, paupers with no land. Enclosed by solid walls at the centre of his fields and grazing lands, the powerful clan chief reigned. They all worked very hard: the austere clan chief wouldn't have disdained to join his family in ploughing the fields, harvesting, or in the gathering of the grapes. However, when the Senate met, he put on his white toga with a red border and went into the city. His responsibility as the head of one of the basic units of the state made it necessary for him to participate in the meetings which decided their common destiny.

The Roman Republic

Although a little faded, on an ancient wall can still be read the 2,000-year-old inscription: N. BARCHA. II V. V. B. O. V. F. And further along, another one which is just as faded: TV DE CONTRA ROG. DEB. ARTOR. And so even then there were abbreviations and puzzling letters. In fact, the first phrase should be read: N(umerium) Barcha(M) II (two) v(irum) v(irum) b(onum),

o(ro) v(os) f(aciatis). Which means, 'Elect Numerio Barcha for he is a good man'. Therefore this writing is electoral propaganda. The other writing maintains: Tu de contra rog(are) deb(es) Artor(ium): 'You should vote for Artorius instead'. Thus in the Roman world they used a sort of electoral posters and propaganda just as we do today during general and local elections.

THE PEOPLE AND THE NEW KING

In the year 509 B.C. – according to tradition – a popular uprising expelled the last king, Tarquin the Proud. Rome became a republic. (In Latin, *res publica* means 'the thing belonging to everybody'.)

The territory of Rome, its affairs and its governments were no longer a 'private affair', belonging to the king.

All the free citizens, the Roman people, became the new 'king'. United in an assembly they elected the magistrates who usually governed the city for a year.

Above left: electoral publicity written on a wall in Pompeii, on the right, ancient Roman Republican money; a bronze coin from the fourth to the third century B.C. with a winged horse and the inscription ROMANOM and two coins from the third century B.C.

CLASS	TAX	CENTURIES AND VOTES	ARMOUR
I	10,000 coins	98	Defence: helmet, breast-plate, metal shield, back-plate. Attack: short sword, dagger, spear. N.B. 18 centuries were horsemen.
II	75,000 coins	22	Defence: as before but without breast-plate and with a wooden shield. Attack: spear and sword.
III	50,000 coins	20	Defence: as before but without back-plate. Attack: as before.
IV	25,000 coins	22	Defence: a rectangular shield. Attack: lances and javelins.
V	12,500 coins	30	Defence: none, or a small round shield ot leather and wood. Attack: bows and arrows or slings for hurling missiles.
VI	Coins: none	1	Excluded from military service.

Roman society changes

In the most ancient Roman times, the people who counted were the 'patres', the noble clan chiefs who had always ruled alongside the king.

However as Rome consolidated and extended its dominion with its armies and grew rich with trade and industry, others became more important. These were the merchants, the makers of arms, and those who supplied the needs of the army.

As compensation after a victorious war they were given pieces of land which they exploited and thus grew rich.

These new 'men of power' were rarely of noble origin or patricians. On the contrary they were often common people. Their riches did not consist of just fields, grazing land and livestock (this was the typical heritage of the patriarchal families), but most of all, in ready cash, thousands of bronze coins, which were the oldest Roman money.

It was they who made Rome prosperous, even lending money to the state to finance the wars, but politically they had no influence: it was obvious that they wanted to change this state of affairs.

The consul presides over the meeting to elect his successor. The male Roman citizens, divided by classes and by

The Centurial Assemblies

The Romans were always trying to be practical and realistic: nobility from birth was all very well, but riches were more important. From this began the simple principle: the more one had, the more one gave to the state. The Roman people was thus divided into five classes, as we can see on the diagram (bottom left), plus a sixth, the 'proletarii', people whose only wealth was their abundance of sons (proles).

The main obligation of a citizen, whether rich or not, was to provide soldiers and equipment to the army.

According to their wealth, every class had to provide a certain number of centuries (bodies of 100 fully equipped fighters). In exchange they received greater power. In fact when it came to electing magistrates or approving laws every century had a vote. So for example, those belonging to the first class, the richest, armed 98 centuries and therefore had 98 votes: this was more than the votes of all the other classes which had 95. The general assembly of the Roman people in which the citizens participated, arranged in their various centuries, took the name of the Centurial Assembly.

centuries, are split up into 'folds' which are built of wood and have but one single exit.

The election of the consuls

The Centurial Assembly had been called according to the law. In the largest open space in Rome, the Field of Mars, the 193 centuries gathered together. The consul elected the previous year was about to stand down and he was overseeing the important meeting, sitting on the elegant chair of gilt and ivory, symbol of the great dignity of the magistrates. Everybody knew who the candidates were. They had almost a month to get themselves known and to win votes with speeches, and by writing propaganda on the walls. Every century had discussed it at length and decided on the name of one candidate. At the end of the voting the count was made and then the heralds proclaimed the two newly elected consuls who, for a year, in war or peace, would be the most powerful people in Rome.

At the end of his time as consul, a man might continue his political career as a proconsul, taking command of a province. As Rome declined, many proconsuls used their office to line their own pockets or as a base for conquest, but at the height of Rome's power, the proconsuls were very often fair and conscientious governors.

THE PATRICIANS AND PLEBS: A LONG STRUGGLE FOR EQUALITY

Think about initials. The most famous are the initials of the Roman Republic S.P.Q.R. which meant: Senatus Populus Que Romanus – the Senate and the Roman People. The unity of these two represented the power of Rome.

The former was made up of the powerful and noble clan chiefs of ancient origin and the highest magistrates after they had left office. The latter, through the assembly, elected their magistrates and approved all the most important decisions. However, this unity between the senate and the people, between all citizens who made up the Roman people, was a conquest (which was never total) won after years of struggle.

Patricians and Plebs

It is often thought that the 'noble patricians' and the 'humble plebs' of Rome were simply the rich and poor in the city. In reality it was different. For example, even among the plebs there were people who had grown rich enough to enter into the first two classes of the six into which the citizens of Rome were divided.

At the same time we know of instances of patricians, descendants of the patres who had become noble by helping Romulus and the first kings to make Rome great (and had taken the best land), who were reduced to living in modest conditions.

Therefore it was not simply a division of rich and poor, but something else: they lived side by side, they helped each other in their daily business, and during war fought side by side. But patricians and plebs never managed to blend into one compact body.

Conditions of inferiority

Naturally, most patricians, the owners of land, led a fairly comfortable existence. They lived in lovely houses in the city or more often in the country. They had servants, slaves and teachers for their children. They also had all rights: not only could they vote like the plebs but only they could be elected consuls or magistrates. Even after

Right: a view of a road in a common part of Rome with workshops, people working and children playing.
Below: a model reconstruction of an apartment house, an 'insula', in Ostia.

the setting up of the centurial assemblies they continued to hold curial assemblies which only patricians could participate in.

Most of the plebs led a less comfortable existence. They mostly lived in the city in very squalid areas: in houses with several storeys – called 'insulae' – in tiny and uncomfortable apartments; shops, craftworks, laboratories of every kind were on the lower floors: many plebs were craftsmen, shop-keepers and small traders.

However plebs were also an organised community. They had their official representatives (not recognised by the patricians or the Senate). They met in Tribal Assemblies where they voted on a one man one vote basis.

The most difficult thing for the plebs to tolerate was the condition of inferiority in which they were kept.

Struggles and successes

The plebs fought, worked and voted for the magistrates but they could not be elected. Like everybody else they sometimes needed the tribunals and tribunes but these were in the hands of the patricians and only they could become judges and knew the law by heart. There was no longer a law valid and clear for everyone. A pleb could not marry a member of the nobility. When lands were allotted they all went to the patricians. Added to this, the frequent wars which Rome fought often impoverished the plebs. They fought when there was good weather,

when the common peasants had to abandon their fields and craftsmen commoners had to close their workshops. They all got into debt to maintain their families. When they found themselves unable to pay back their debts they could be sold as slaves or even killed. From the fifth century B.C. the open struggle between the patricians, who defended the rights and privileges of their class, and the plebs who fought for equality, racked Roman society. As can be seen from the table on page 31, at the end of the struggle the common people achieved equality with the patricians. But a real and proper union was never made.

Family Life

The household was the centre of life for many Romans, and the oldest male within a family had *patria potestas* over the lives and property of his family – that is, he had supreme authority. His wife, like all women, was regarded as someone who should be kept in a state of lifelong subjugation. When she married, she passed straight from her father's authority to her husband's, and when he died, she could be commanded by her son. The son, by contrast, could one day hope to be *pater familias* himself, and as such have absolute authority over his wife and children, to the extent that he could have his sons executed, sold into slavery or formally expelled from the family. Such actions were probably rare, but they did reinforce the father's authority.

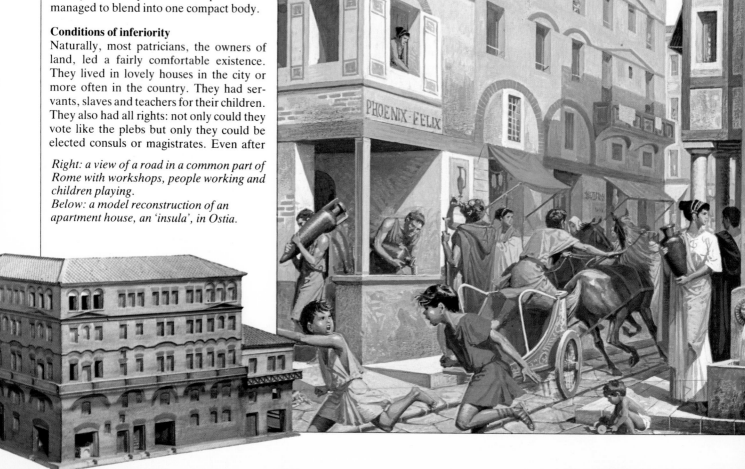

A view of a funerary stele from the first century B.C. showing the inside of a butcher's shop.

WHO RULED IN ROME

In the sketch below we can see how the leadership of Rome was made up. The centurial assemblies elected the magistrates who governed the Republic, the two consuls with full power in war and peace, the praetors who administered justice, and the censors who made up the lists of citizens according to the censuses. The consuls were elected with the approval of the Senate which was the real power in Roman politics; and the support of the curial assemblies, the assemblies of the 30 Curias into which the people were divided. The Tribal Assemblies, made up of the city's tribes and later also those from the countryside, elected the aediles who took care of public services, and the quaestors who took care of the tax entries. The people's assembly elected its representatives, the Tribunes of the People. In cases of necessity the consuls could elect a dictator who had unlimited power.

Underneath this ruling class was the mass of peasants and slaves.

STEPS TOWARDS EQUALITY

6th–5th century B.C. – The centurial assemblies, now based on wealth and no longer on noble birth, allow the common people of Rome to become Roman citizens. If they grew rich they could pass from an inferior class to a superior one.

494 B.C. – After having threatened to leave the city (to break the agreements of collaboration with the patricians), the magistrates of the common people are recognised. These were the powerful people's tribunes who were inviolable and sacred and from whom a 'no' could block any decision contrary to their interests.

450 B.C. – A commission of ten men (Decemviri) who had full powers established the first written Roman law. It was the law of the Twelve Tablets, written on twelve bronze plates and displayed in the forum. This was a victory for the common people; the patrician judges could no longer dispense justice as they saw fit.

445 B.C. – The Canuleian tribunal approves the law which allows marriages between nobility and common people.

367–366 B.C. – The magistrates Lucinius Stolo and Sextus Lateranus approve some very important laws: admission of the common people to the position of consul (later one of the two consuls had to be of plebeian origin): a reduction of debts; a limit of 125 hectares of conquered territory could be privately owned, almost always by patricians.

366 B.C. – Common people can also be elected to the position of aedile.

356 B.C. – A pleb can also become the dictator.

339 B.C. – The delicate office of censor is also opened to the common people.

337 B.C. – A common person can become praetor, i.e. judge.

326 B.C. – The law allowing the creditor to make his debtor a slave was abolished (they were normally poor common people).

302 B.C. – Common people are also allowed to become priests.

SENATE

DICTATOR

CURIAL ASSEMBLY

CENTURIAL ASSEMBLY

CONSUL

CONSUL

TRIBAL ASSEMBLY

PRAETOR

CENSOR

AEDILE

QUAESTOR

PEOPLE'S TRIBUNES

PEASANTS

SLAVES

PLEBS

Rome at War

The arms and equipment of a legionary. Among his defensive arms were: a metallic helmet with a neck guard and cheek guards, often decorated with feathers or with horse hairs; a large rectangular shield made of wood and covered in leather reinforced with metal decorations; armour which during battle was worn over a leather tunic or chain mail; leg protectors. Among the offensive weapons were 'piles', two long wooden spears with iron tips (these were hurled at the beginning of the battle and stuck in the shields of the enemy who then had to pull them out or do away with the shields, lessening their defence); the 'gladius', a short sword; a dagger, as a last resort. The individual legionary carried food for two or three days and water supplies; a mess tin and a spoon and a little pot to cook the cereal pulp, the 'puls', which was his basic food; three sticks and a sheet (usually animal skins) with which to put up his tent; a scythe for cutting down the crops around the camp; a spade or pick to dig a ditch or build a defensive fence around the camp.

Here is a Roman legionary, who was one of the main protagonists of Roman history. He was usually a peasant, often dragged away from his fields and sent off here and there: Italy, Spain, Northern Europe, Africa, the East. With his equipment on his back, weighing from 35'to 40 kilogrammes, he normally marched 35 kilometres a day and this became 40 if a forced march was necessary. And when he reached his destination he worked for another four or five hours to set up camp.

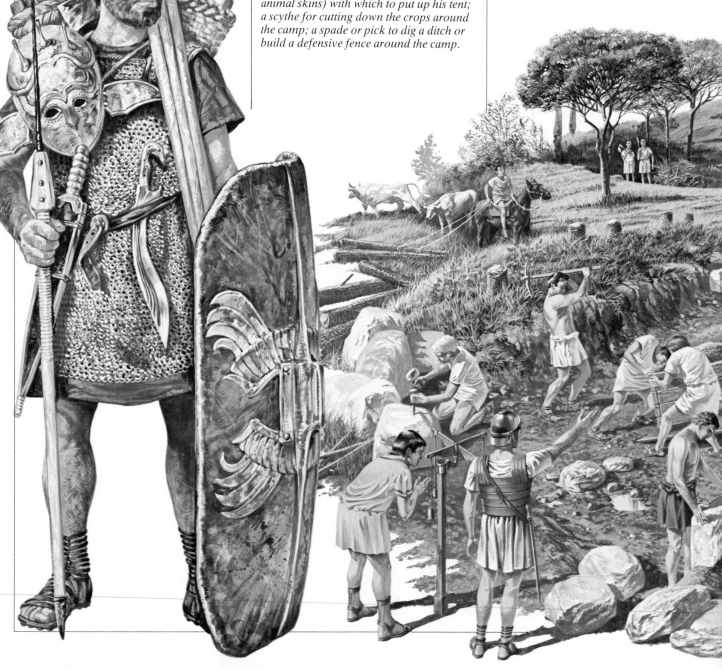

MASTERS OF THE MEDITERRANEAN IN 350 YEARS

After the expulsion of the last king, the Republic of Rome was at war almost every year.

Let's have a look at the series of wars which Rome sustained over three centuries and which led to the conquest of an empire.

The conquest of Latium (509 to 390 B.C.)

From 509 to 396 B.C. Rome fought against its neighbours, the powerful Etruscans, the other cities in Latium united in a league (the Latin League), the Aequines and the Volsci. This struggle ended only in 396 B.C. when the Romans took and destroyed the Etruscan city of Veii, the most serious rival for supremacy in Latium.

A few years later, the Celts or Gauls of Northern Italy, during the course of an incursion, beat the Romans (390 B.C.) and

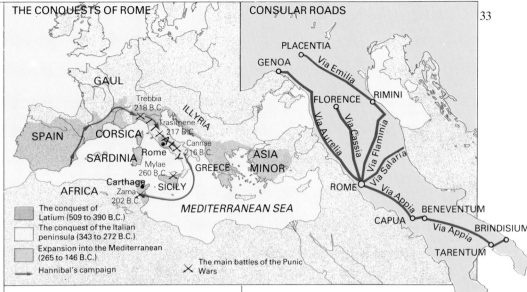

Above left: The conquests of Rome from 509 B.C. to 146 B.C., and the route taken by Hannibal of Carthage during his campaign. Above right: The principal roads of the Roman Empire in Italy.

occupied Rome. The payment of a huge ransom and a military turnabout was enough to send the Gauls back north, but there was a score to settle.

The conquest of the Italian peninsula (343 to 272 B.C.)

Three terrible wars and fifty years of uninterrupted fighting: this was the price that the Romans paid to defeat another powerful pretender for the domination of Italy – the Samnite people. Beaten and humiliated on many occasions, the Romans finally obtained a decisive victory at Sentinum in the Marche Region (195 B.C.). Their dominion extended over a territory including Tuscany, Umbria, Marche, Abruzzi and Campania. Then between 280 and 272 B.C. by beating Pyrrhus, king of Epirus, the Romans extended their dominion over the territory of Magna Grecia.

Expansion in the Mediterranean (165 to 146 B.C.)

The Phoenician city of Carthage which dominated the Western Mediterranean clashed with Rome in a battle that was to prove decisive for the history of the European and Middle Eastern civilisations.

The three Punic wars gave Rome supremacy over the Mediterranean and also over Spain, the northern coast of Africa, Greece and the East. Among other events of the Punic wars were the conquest of Cisalpine Gaul (or Northern Italy), Greece and Syria.

Rome was now the capital of an empire with its centre in the Mediterranean.

Wars and roads

When the war was over, the soldiers often became builders, especially of roads. These were mainly built for military reasons. In 'slow wars', like those of ancient times, having good roads, along which to move legions, supplies and war machines speedily, became a decisive element. Thanks to the building and firm control of their roads, the Roman army was able to move up to three times as fast as its strongest enemies. Naturally these great roads, which were built during wars or as consequences of them, then became channels for the spreading of Roman culture.

The ancient Roman consular roads (called this because they took the name of the consul who coordinated their construction) are still today the backbone of Italian road networks, and to a large extent European ones as well.

As far as possible, the Romans let nothing stand in their way when building roads. They made them as straight as possible, using viaducts and aqueducts to keep them straight. The roads were measured off at regular distances so that the traveller would know exactly how far he was from the Golden Milestone in the Forum in Rome.

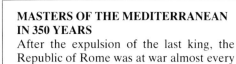

To build their roads the Romans filled a ditch with stones and then covered them with pebbles, the smaller ones at the top. They then covered it all with a layer of flat stones which were polygonal in shape. The roads which were almost always straight were from four to six metres wide.

EITHER CARTHAGE OR ROME

A year before the monarchy fell in 510 B.C. Rome made a pact with Carthage, the African Phoenician city which for centuries had ruled the seas from Greece to the Pillars of Hercules (Gibraltar) and which even dared to send ships beyond them. The pact was renewed in 348 B.C. on more or less the same conditions. Rome recognised Carthaginian rights to trade and pirate throughout the Mediterranean. Carthage promised not to enter the Tyrrhenian Sea and attack Latin cities or any which had a pact or alliance with Rome. This seemed like a very good agreement, but in fact it only lasted a few decades.

Then furious armed conflict broke out between the two cities – the three Punic wars – which for 118 years held history in the balance. Either Carthage or Rome: only one could dominate the future development of the west.

The power of Carthage

Carthage was founded about a century before Rome on the African coast where Tunis stands today. It was a Phoenician city, mainly seafaring and commercial and dedicated to constant expansion on the seas, in the search for distant lands.

At the same time, it was a rich industrial and agricultural city. After two and a half centuries of good neighbourly relations Carthage had even occupied Sicily through its commercial expansion. At the same time Rome had its sights set on this island, both because it was an excellent grain-producing area and because it occupied a vital position for the control of commercial and military routes in the Mediterranean. A clash was inevitable.

At first, the Sicilians accepted a Carthaginian garrison when they were attacked, but then they appealed to Rome for assistance. The result was the Punic Wars.

THE FIRST PUNIC WAR (264 TO 241 B.C.)

264 B.C. – The struggle for Sicily became intense. Victorious on the land, the Romans occupied the western part as far as Agrigento (261 B.C.).

260 B.C. – The Romans land near Carthage and are totally routed.

250 – 249 B.C. – Alternating victories and defeats for both sides.

241 B.C. – A decisive naval victory for Rome near the Aegates islands. Rome obtains Sicily, Sardinia, Corsica.

229 – 222 B.C. – Rome occupies part of Yugoslavia.
In Italy at Clastidium (Casteggio Pavia) they defeat the Gauls, occupying one of their capital cities, Mediolanum (Milan).
South of the Po they formed the colonies of Placentia (Piacenza), Mutina (Modena) and Bononia (Bologna).

Here is a view of two types of ship which at different times made a great contribution to the Roman war effort. The Romans made innovations to their ships which rendered them more efficient in battle. On the 'deceres' (left) they mounted a tower at the prow and at the stern which gave the archers an elevated shooting position which made them better both for attack and defence.

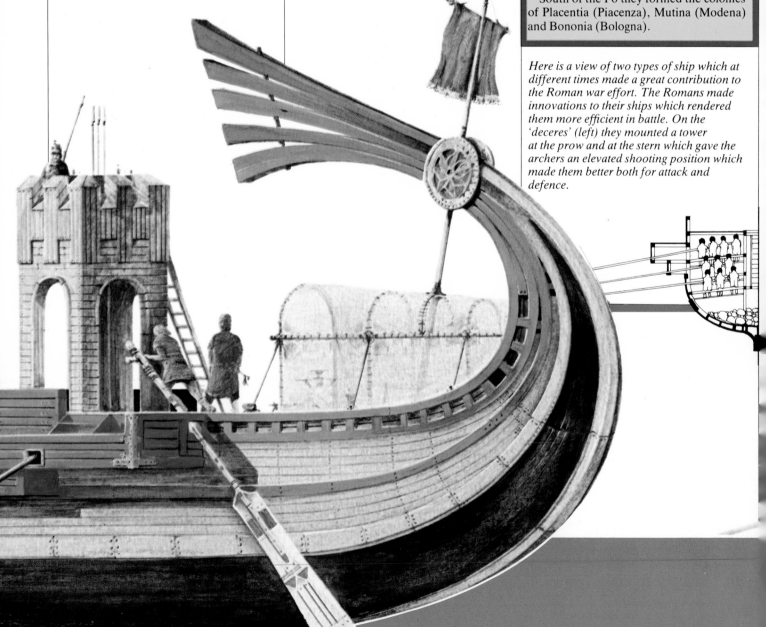

War on the seas

In the first war between Rome and Carthage, the Roman military machine was sorely put to the test.

The situation was completely new. A land power like Rome was challenging a sea power like Carthage.

On the island of Sicily the Roman legions gained important victories but they didn't win the war. Carthage had to be beaten on the seas. The naval battles in ancient times almost always took place in the same way. With their oarsmen working at maximum speed the ships tried to ram the enemy's flank with their prow. Because it was armed with a strong rostrum or bronze spike, the prow smashed into the enemy flank and sank the ship. At the moment of impact the sailors and soldiers aboard ship jumped on to the enemy ship and fought them hand to hand.

After long experience the Carthaginians were much more skilful than the Romans at this kind of battle: launching their ships at great speed, stopping them suddenly, or putting them crossways to avoid being speared and carrying out all sorts of manoeuvres in restricted spaces at great speed. But at Mylae the Carthaginians were amazed to see something new.

On the sea, as on the land

The largest Roman ships were as big as those of the Carthaginians; in fact it is said that they were copied from a Carthaginian ship washed ashore after a storm. They were about 40 metres long and could carry 400 fighting men. They were made heavier at the prow however by a sort of drawbridge, which was connected to a mast and equipped with hooks in such a way that it could be lowered either to the left or to the right. It was called a 'crow' and is said to have been installed by the chief admiral, the consul Caius Duilius.

In the battle the Roman ships adopted a new tactic. They attacked from the side, shattering the oars of the enemy ship, immobilising it (the Roman rowers pulled in their oars at the right time). At the same time the 'crow' was lowered on to the bridge, joining the two ships and creating a wide gang-plank for the infantry to cross. The battle became similar to a land encounter at which the Roman infantry were better. This was really nothing revolutionary. In fact the 'crows' weighed down the ship, unbalancing it at the front, thus making manoeuvres difficult, and they were soon abandoned without regret. But this 'innovation' was enough to give Rome supremacy on the seas.

This quinquereme led the attack in the first naval battles fought by the Romans and was equipped to transform the encounter into a land battle. In fact at the prow they mounted a 'crow', a sort of drawbridge with hooks at one end. Attached to a mast by ropes, it could be dropped on to the bridge of enemy ships.

In a quinquereme, the oars were in three banks. The top two were pulled by two oarsmen, the third by one. In the deceres the top oar was pulled by four oarsmen and the bottom two by three each.

THE ARMY IN THE FIELD
Seventeen nightmarish years.

Between 218 and 201 B.C. – the period of the second Punic war – mighty Rome ran the most serious risk of its entire history. It lost numerous battles and in many of them was totally routed. In the end however, it won and its legions grew famous everywhere as being invincible. What was the secret?

Citizen and Soldier

From 17 to 60 the Roman citizen was also a soldier. Until the age of 45 he could be enrolled and sent to fight in the front lines. The older ones (46 to 60 years) made up the reserves used for looking after the arms and for the defence of the city.

Giving military service was considered so important that no-one could present himself as a candidate for public office unless he had served as a soldier or an officer for at least ten years.

The ingredients of invincibility

Training, organisation, discipline: these were the ingredients which gave the Roman armies the well-earned reputation of being invincible.

The young men were trained in the Field of Mars, a large space outside the city walls, under the eyes of the public (to encourage them to do their best). There the new recruits learned to march, learned hand-to-hand combat and especially how to carry out collective manoeuvres with absolute and split-second precision and, most important, obedience to the orders of the 'centurion', the officer who guided the action of the units containing from 80 to 100 men, the ancient century.

A bust of the Carthaginian army leader, Hannibal.

Below, an African infantryman.

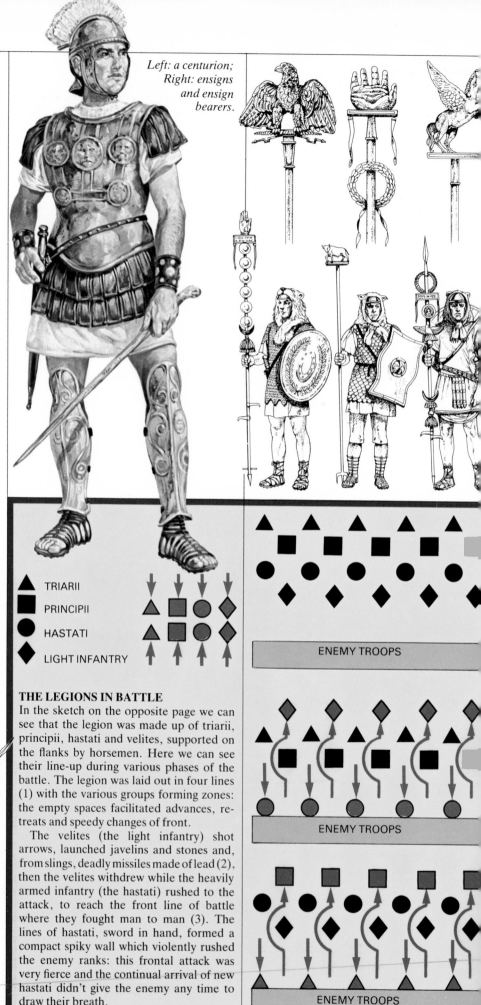

Left: a centurion; Right: ensigns and ensign bearers.

▲ TRIARII
■ PRINCIPII
● HASTATI
◆ LIGHT INFANTRY

ENEMY TROOPS

ENEMY TROOPS

ENEMY TROOPS

THE LEGIONS IN BATTLE

In the sketch on the opposite page we can see that the legion was made up of triarii, principii, hastati and velites, supported on the flanks by horsemen. Here we can see their line-up during various phases of the battle. The legion was laid out in four lines (1) with the various groups forming zones: the empty spaces facilitated advances, retreats and speedy changes of front.

The velites (the light infantry) shot arrows, launched javelins and stones and, from slings, deadly missiles made of lead (2), then the velites withdrew while the heavily armed infantry (the hastati) rushed to the attack, to reach the front line of battle where they fought man to man (3). The lines of hastati, sword in hand, formed a compact spiky wall which violently rushed the enemy ranks: this frontal attack was very fierce and the continual arrival of new hastati didn't give the enemy any time to draw their breath.

The fighting unit: the legion

At the time of the Punic wars, a legion contained 4,200 soldiers. Later on the number was increased to between 5,000 and 6,000 heavy infantry flanked by a minimum of 900 cavalry.

To facilitate movement in the field the legion was subdivided into cohorts (usually 10) and every cohort into 'maniples'. In their turn maniples were divided into more mobile units: centuries, once of 100 men and then of a number from 80 to 150.

The centurion, the officer who fought at the right flank of the front line, commanded the century.

At the other end of the front line, another officer ('tesserarius') transmitted orders to his own men and to the centurion of the century alongside.

At the last place on the left of the last line there was a third officer who communicated orders coming from behind the lines and saw to the removing of wounded colleagues.

In the centre of the array was the 'aquilifer' or 'signifer' (the bearer of the eagle or the legion's ensign) and the herald with a trumpet, and they coordinated the action of the various centuries, maniples and cohorts either with movements of the ensign or by trumpet blasts.

The action of the two legions which made up the nucleus of a Roman army was directed by the tribunes or by the superior officers and the consul, the army leader who had supreme command and total responsibility for the battle.

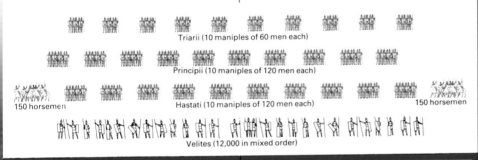

Triarii (10 maniples of 60 men each)

Principii (10 maniples of 120 men each)

150 horsemen   Hastati (10 maniples of 120 men each)   150 horsemen

Velites (12,000 in mixed order)

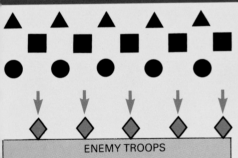

ENEMY TROOPS

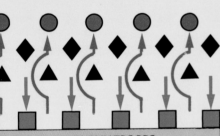

ENEMY TROOPS

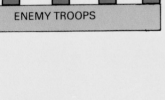

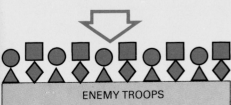

ENEMY TROOPS

Taking advantage of the disarray, the hastati withdrew using the corridors they had opened up in the enemy ranks, to rest and regroup. Meantime other heavily armed infantry, the principii, advanced; the deadly pressure on the enemy was not only kept but it was increased by these new forces (4).

Meanwhile the Roman cavalry launched its attack from behind, surprising the enemy.

All the principii withdrew from the fighting. They rested and prepared for a new assault. Meanwhile, other heavily armed infantry, the expert veterans (the so-called triarii) took over from the principii and renewed the hammering attack (5). If these attacks hadn't overcome the enemy's resistance then this 'merry-go-round' of hastati, principii, triarii, began all over again. In the final phases of the battle (6) all the forces united to launch the final offensive.

It was these tactics that made the Roman armies almost invincible for hundreds of years; these and the superb discipline of the Roman soldiers. Life was no doubt tough for the soldiers, but they were trained to accept that, and also that they were fighting for the glory of Rome, something that had been drummed into them since childhood.

It was only when the Roman civilisation became corrupt and decadent, many hundreds of years later, that the Roman soldiers became less daunting to opposing troops.

THE SECOND PUNIC WAR (218 TO 201 B.C.)

237–226 B.C. – Carthage conquers territory in Spain. Rome takes over the region on the other side of the Pyrenees to form a sort of protective 'cushion'.

219 B.C. – The Carthaginians' general, Hannibal, conquers the Spanish city of Saguntum which was allied to Rome. War is declared.

218 B.C. – Hannibal launches a surprise attack against the Romans who are ready to land in Africa, with his whole army (50,000 men, 9,000 horses, 37 elephants). He crosses the Pyrenees and then the Alps. In Italy he defeats the Romans at the rivers Ticino and Trebbia, near Lake Trasimene.

216 B.C. – Hannibal has been in Italy for almost two years. In August the Roman legions give battle but they are destroyed at Cannae: this is Rome's most disastrous defeat. Of 86,000 men, 50,000 were killed.

215–207 B.C. – Hannibal is still in Italy and constitutes a serious threat, but Rome changes strategy. Instead of attacking him directly they cut off his supply lines and defeat the allies that he has made in the meantime. In this way the Roman legions conquer Spain and Greece and acquire Sicily.

207 B.C. – A reinforcement army led by Hasdrubal, Hannibal's brother, is destroyed near the river Metauro. For the first time the Romans employ the tactic of 'encircling and enclosing' which they had learnt to their cost from Hannibal himself.

204 B.C. – Rome on the attack. The Roman general Publius Cornelius Scipio lands in Africa. Hannibal is called back to defend his city, Carthage.

202 B.C. – At Zama, about 70 kilometres from Carthage, Scipio avenges the defeat at Cannae. Hannibal's army is wiped out. Carthage has to sue for peace.

200–180 B.C. – Turning against their ancient enemies who had taken up arms again and recent allies of Hannibal's, the legions expand Roman dominion throughout Spain, northern Italy and modern Yugoslavia, Turkey and Syria. Greece becomes subject to Rome.

'The camp is a second home and for every soldier his tent is his house and the centre of his life.' These words, spoken by a consul, and written down by the Roman historian Livy, show the importance given to the camp. A modern historian adds: 'The Roman camp was one of the greatest military solutions of all time' to a series of problems: it could hold several thousand people, animals, supplies and military machines; the building of a sort of little city, which was fully equipped and didn't have to rely on the outside world, was a solid protection like a fortress which could be set up and taken down in just a few hours . . .

Here we can see this brilliant solution; a typical Roman camp which remained the same for eight to ten centuries.

Alongside we can see how a Roman camp was constructed: 1 Praetorium road; 2 principal road; 3 Praetorium, the square where the general's tent was set up; 4 Praetorium gate; 5 Decuman gate; 6 principal left gate; 7 principal right gate; 8 observation towers; 9 lodgings for the guards; 10 quaestor; 11 higher ranking officers' lodgings; 12 legionaries' lodgings; 13 forum, place for parades; 14 defensive ditches.

THE END OF THE WAR

The Roman camp was so well organised and it responded so well to the needs of the people who lived in it, the legions, that many of them became permanent. The skin tents were replaced by wooden huts and then stone houses, the straight alignment of the roads which crossed each other at right angles was rigorously maintained because it made up a sensible road network. The forum became the main square and in the place of the commander's tents (the Praetorium) was built the government building . . . So this temporary camp became a city. Many modern cities – Padua, Turin, Aosta, and many others – conserved in their centres the geometrical pattern of the Roman camp. This is a significant example of the way in which the legions influenced civilian life long after the war was over, in the lands which up to a short time before had seen them fight.

The Roman dominions

When the war was over, naturally most legionaries went home. The cities they had defeated received different treatment according to the circumstances. Some were welcomed by Rome as allies or confederates which had to pay an annual tribute and keep a Roman garrison to watch over them, but kept all their own laws and systems of government. Other conquered cities obtained even more: in fact their inhabitants could even become 'cives Romani' with full citizens' rights . . . just like the Romans in Rome.

In other cases the territories conquered were placed under the direct administration of Rome and were ruled by a governor.

The provinces were: Sicily first, then Sardinia, Corsica, Spain, Carthage and Africa.

The legionary becomes a colonist

However, some legionaries did not go home at the end of the war. It often happened that as a reward for bravery or long years of faithful military service, they were given a piece of land to cultivate in the newly acquired regions. The 'miles' became a colonist. The land was carefully divided into equal pieces. Loans and help from the state allowed the ex-legionary to build a house, buy plough beasts and tools. It was also through this means that the mighty conqueror Rome spread its civilisation, its ways and its culture. As we shall see further on, this work of 'Romanisation' of the provinces won through war was slow but very deep. It was so deep that present-day Europe and a large part of what we call the West owe their cultural unity to this work.

With the war over, Rome now controlled the entire western Mediterranean. With some territorial gains in the eastern Mediterranean, that sea became virtually a Roman lake. But the acquisition of such an enormous empire put a terrible strain on the Roman political system. However, Rome managed to survive despite a series of intensely bitter civil wars. The final one lasted from 49–30 B.C. and was largely fought between the armies of two of the greatest generals the world has ever known – Pompey and Julius Caesar, who had until then been allies along with another general, Crassus. Caesar was the conqueror of Gaul and Britain and had extended the power of Rome from the Rhine to the Atlantic. At the battle of Pharsalus, Caesar's battle-hardened troops demolished Pompey's forces and Caesar was undisputed master of the Roman world.

The Romans used slaves to bring huge building projects to realisation. Among their greatest works were the aqueducts which distributed water to the cities through a system of siphons, lead pipes which poured water from one level to a lower level. Roman engineers got their huge blocks of stone into place using winches, pulleys and cranes.

THE END OF CARTHAGE (149–146 B.C.)

149 B.C. – According to the peace treaty, the Carthaginians could not make war without Rome's approval. However it was Rome that incited them, or at least stood by and watched some of its African allies stir up war against Carthage. The reason was obvious: a third rapid war would totally destroy their dangerous rival.

146 B.C. – Having found a pretext (Carthage reacted to the incessant harassment which it received from Rome's allies with arms), the Senate ordered two armies to land in Africa and besiege Carthage. The city put up a long and desperate resistance, but in the end it fell. It was razed to the ground. The inhabitants were killed or sold as slaves. The booty was enormous.

In the same year the Romans ended their conquest of Greece and extended their dominions in the East. Rome became the unchallenged master of the Mediterranean. However, Carthage was so well sited that 100 years later it was one of the most prosperous Roman cities in the Mediterranean.

An aerial view of Aosta. The city grew up from a Roman camp in the Augustan era and still almost entirely conserves its fortified Roman walls which are in the form of a quadrilateral with the sides measuring 550 by 690 metres. On the eastern side of the walls there are still some watch towers and the Praetorium gate. The lay-out of the roads which are at perfect right angles also derived from those of the Roman camp.

Every year Julius Caesar is remembered, not only for one day on the anniversary of his birth or death, but for 31 consecutive days. The seventh month of the year, in almost all languages is known as July in honour of Julius 'Caesar'. Many nations also remember Julius Caesar when speaking about their former rulers: the German 'Kaiser' and the Russian 'Tsar' derived from the Roman word Caesar. This is a strange destiny for the man who was the last great man of the republic but didn't want or didn't manage to become the first emperor of the Roman Empire. Julius Caesar did not kill the Roman republic: he just had the courage to bury it,

recognising that it was already dead when he became the single ruler of Rome. He refused several times to have himself declared king. He was not officially king, but he had all the king's powers. The Senate had given him – for life – the powers which in the olden days belonged to the various magistrates, but only for a limited period of time. Julius Caesar was the 'imperator' – that means he commanded all the land and sea forces. Like the old dictator he had the so-called 'imperium Romae' which gave him the power to rule over all citizens and allies. Like the people's tribunes, he had the right to veto, the right to block every decision contrary to his will.

The Golden Era of Imperial Rome

Above, a bust of Caesar, the last great man of the Republic, and one of Augustus, the first real Emperor.
Below, a scene from the battle of Actium, the last great battle between Romans.

The struggle begins again

Twenty-three dagger thrusts – many from old friends – in the middle of the Senate, on the 15th March 44 B.C. ended Caesar's life.

The hands which held the daggers were those of the Roman aristocracy. They believed that with Caesar out of the way, the defunct republic would come back to life. But facts betrayed them. It was then clear that the government of Rome was contended for by 'strong men' who settled all matters of law, institutions and offices, once decided by the people.

The three 'strong men'

There were three strong men and it was obvious that in the end only one would prevail.

Marcus Antonius (Mark Antony): the brave fighter, a friend of Caesar's and his second-in-command in dozens of battles. After Caesar's death, he roused the Romans against the plotters with a famous speech, during which he revealed that a part of the huge heritage of the murdered dictator had been left to the citizens of Rome. The plotters were forced to flee. For several months Mark Antony seemed Caesar's natural heir.

Marcus Aemilius Lepidus: Caesar had held him in high esteem as a brave and capable leader of his cavalry. Moreover he was intelligent and skilful in politics and very rich.

Caius Julius Caesar Octavianus: years later the Senate named him Augustus – that is, the greatest. He was Caesar's great-nephew and had been adopted by him as a son. For this reason he inherited most of his immense riches: so much so that he was able to pay for entire armies. He was only nineteen when Caesar died but he joined in the war with all the rest.

A new alliance of three

These three didn't come to loggerheads immediately, in fact they made an agreement. This second triumvirate was magistrature recognised by the Senate, unlike the unofficial one that Caesar had shared with Pompey and Crossus. Its official task was to save Rome by any means. The first thing to do was catch up with Caesar's murderers, who had set up an army in Greece. They were overtaken at Philippi in Macedonia where they were completely wiped out. Then for the good of Rome, the triumvirate had to divide the power: Antony was given the East and Transalpine Gaul which he had conquered together with Caesar; Lepidus was given Africa where he would be able to grow rich at his pleasure; Octavian got

Rome and the rest of the West – the centre of power.

Each one was to do away with his enemies as he saw fit.

Octavian Augustus: the winner

The contest was soon restricted to the two most warlike, Antony and Octavian. The former fell in love with the beautiful queen whom Caesar had put on the throne of Egypt – Cleopatra.

For her Antony rejected his wife Octavia, the sister of Octavian. He gave her 'jewels' which were not his but Rome's; jewels like Phoenicia, Cyprus, part of Arabia, Cilicia and Palestine! By her he had sons whom he named his heirs. It was not hard for Caesar's nephew to get consent to declare war, not on Antony but on Cleopatra. Octavian did not want to be held responsible for a third civil war after those of Marius with Sulla and Pompey with Caesar. But the third civil war broke out just the same. The two adversaries gave battle off Actium in the Ionian sea (31 B.C.). It was an enormous naval battle! Five hundred large ships on Antony's side, 400 on Octavian's side and more than 200,000 men against each other. Defeated, Antony and Cleopatra fled and then killed themselves. Egypt became the private property of Octavian. The Senate gave Octavian the prize which crowned the glory of the victorious general. At Actium was born the Roman empire which was to govern the world for another 500 years.

Augustus brought peace, order and prosperity. A proper civil service was created to run the Empire, giving good government to the provinces, as well as to Rome. New roads were built and industry and commerce were encouraged. Augustus also reduced the power of the army by reducing its numbers and distributing it over the frontier provinces. In Italy, the only military presence was the emperor's personal bodyguard, one thousand men in all.

EXPANSION OF THE ROMAN EMPIRE

ATLANTIC OCEAN · BRITAIN · Rhine · GERMANY · PANNONIA · GAUL · Po · DACIA · BLACK SEA · Danube · DALMATIA · THRACE · SPAIN · Rome · MACEDONIA · ASIA MINOR · GREECE · MAURITANIA · NUMIDIA · MEDITERRANEAN SEA · AFRICA · CYRENAICA · EGYPT

The Empire under Augustus

The height of the Roman Empire

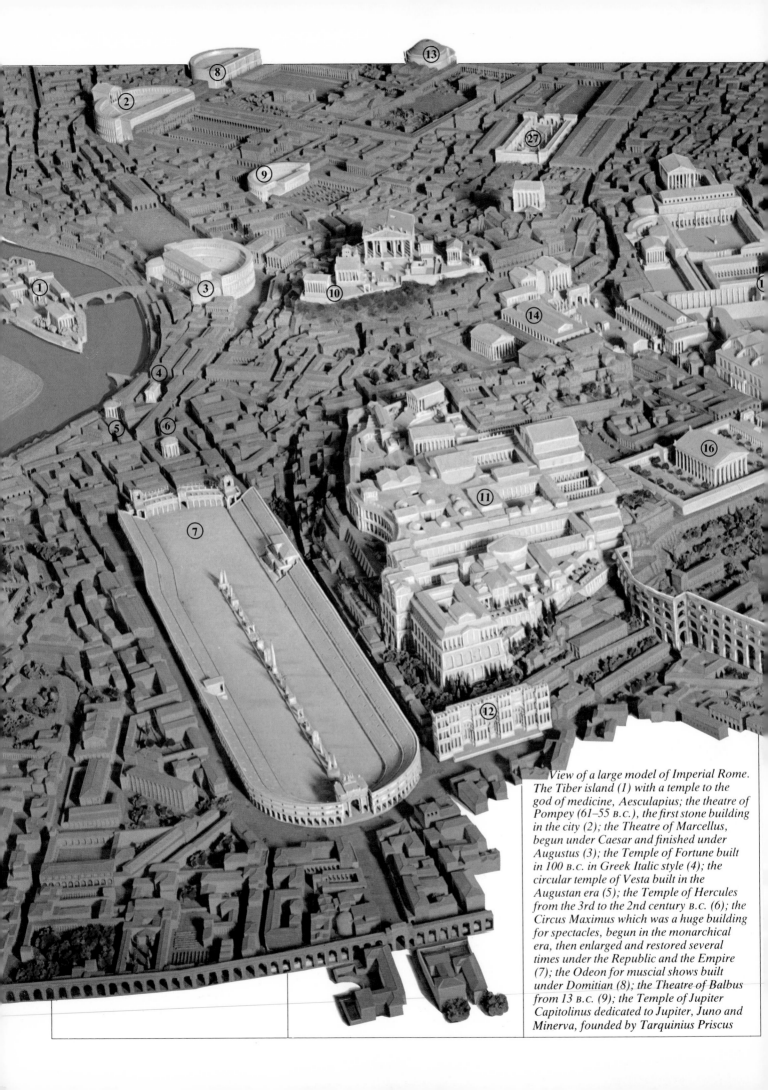

View of a large model of Imperial Rome. The Tiber island (1) with a temple to the god of medicine, Aesculapius; the theatre of Pompey (61–55 B.C.), the first stone building in the city (2); the Theatre of Marcellus, begun under Caesar and finished under Augustus (3); the Temple of Fortune built in 100 B.C. in Greek Italic style (4); the circular temple of Vesta built in the Augustan era (5); the Temple of Hercules from the 3rd to the 2nd century B.C. (6); the Circus Maximus which was a huge building for spectacles, begun in the monarchical era, then enlarged and restored several times under the Republic and the Empire (7); the Odeon for muscial shows built under Domitian (8); the Theatre of Balbus from 13 B.C. (9); the Temple of Jupiter Capitolinus dedicated to Jupiter, Juno and Minerva, founded by Tarquinius Priscus

In Rome there was a famous temple dedicated to the god Janus. This god was shown with two faces, one at the front and one at the back. He was the protector of the beginnings of life and of the year (January comes from his name). He was the god who guarded the doors of the houses, which joined the inside to the outside. He was the god who reconciled opposites. For this reason he was also the god of war and peace: the doors of his temple were closed during times of peace and left open during times of war.

After Augustus had celebrated his magnificent triumph the doors to the temple of Janus were closed. Augustus governed for 42 years (from 29 B.C. to A.D. 14). The Senate nominated him 'princeps' (prince) This title meant that he had the right to intervene in any discussion in the Senate, and he even had the right to be the first to speak. Augustus's decisions were always decisive.

The wars of those years were fought in far-off inhospitable barbarian lands, to extend or reinforce the borders of the empire. The Roman armies were stationed in the provinces. Therefore in Italy and the regions which were conquered first, the impression was not that of living under an iron-fisted military monarchy but that of finally living in a golden age. The bloody years of the civil wars were over and now the Romans contentedly felt that peace ruled the world. People felt that they could finally breathe easily.

The building 'boom'

Especially in Rome, it seemed that the only armed men about were the praetorians, the chosen and personal guard of the princeps, who also did normal police work. It was much more common to see teams of bricklayers, plumbers, stone cutters, mosaic designers, decorators and manual workers. Then there were also technicians to oversee the raising of scaffolding and engineers who built incredible machines for raising enormous weights. Cranes of the time worked with the strength of slaves and ingenious wheels, levers and cogs.

Everywhere there was a rush to build, brighten up, decorate and erect houses and monuments, public buildings and gardens, thermal baths, circuses and theatres. The same thing happened in other cities. This building boom provided work for an enormous number of people and made some very rich.

It is interesting that in the year that the Colosseum was completed, A.D. 80, the cities of Pompeii and Heraculaneum were destroyed when Vesuvius erupted. The layers of ash and pumice choked the citizens and buried the towns, preserving a sad but fascinating record of what Roman life was like at this time.

and inaugurated in 509 B.C. (10); the monumental complex of the Palatine where important emperors lived and where there was a stadium (11); the Septizonium, a colonnaded façade erected by Septimius Severus (12); the Pantheon, the best preserved temple in Rome, begun in 27 B.C. and enlarged under Hadrian in A.D. 118 to 125 (13); the area of the Roman Forum which for centuries was the centre of all activities; in the Imperial era the Imperial Forum was added (14, 15); the temple built by the emperor Elagabulus and named after the sun god (16), with the nearby arch of Titus from B.C. 71; the Basilica of Maxentius or Constantine erected in A.D. 306–312 (17); the Temple of Venus in Rome built by Hadrian A.D. 135 and restored by Maxentius in A.D. 307 (18); the Constantine

Arch from A.D. 315 built to celebrate the victory of Constantine over Maxentius (19); the Claudian aqueduct from the 4th to the 3rd century B.C. (20); the Temple of Serapis from the 2nd to the 3rd century A.D. (21); the Constantine baths (22); the Flavian amphitheatre or Colosseum begun in A.D. 72 in the place where the pool of Nero's Domus Aurea was situated, and finished in A.D. 80: it was used for gladiator fights, animal hunts and mock sea fights (23); the Temple of Claudius built in the first century A.D. (24); the Baths of Titus opened in A.D. 80 (25); the Ludas Magnas where the gladiators were housed, built by Domitian (26); the Porticus Divorum erected by Domitian in honour of Vespasian and Titus, and the nearby temple which might have been built by the Emperor Hadrian (27).

CHANGES IN SOCIETY

What are we to think of a society which had an average of two to three slaves for every free citizen (obviously some had none and others had dozens) and which celebrated feasts for up to 200 days a year? Two thousand years ago we might have heard questions like 'Do these Romans ever work?'

In fact the Pax Romana brought benefits to everyone, but most of all to the Romans. The empire was working like a huge digestive system with Rome as the stomach.

The chain of prosperity

The chain of prosperity started in the most remote provinces in the empire. About 60 years after Augustus, Romans even began to go and get precious silk from China, and the Far East.

A tide of caravans of donkeys, camels, horses, ox-drawn wagons and heavily laden slaves brought everything to the Mediterranean ports and the Roman cities of northern Europe . . . from minerals to wood, from oil to wine, grain and fruit, cloths and jewels, racehorses and slaves for work. Ships filled to bursting arrived at Ostia, Naples, Brindisi and Rome and caravans with military escorts against bandits continually poured into Rome. They came in by night so as not to disturb the daily activity. The Romans then protested about the noise which the animals' hooves and the nailed sandals of the bearers and the cart wheels made on the road, disturbing their sleep. The provinces paid a much higher price for protection and for being swept up in this tide of civil progress which Rome had started off.

When Roman well-being was most widespread the Romans loved to surround themselves with beautiful things, even those articles needed for everyday use. So a great impulse was given to craftwork and the so-called minor arts. The Romans became expert at incorporating into precious stone mythological scenes and portraits, at working silver and gold, at producing artistic ceramics and glasswork. Alongside we can see a glass flask from the second or the third century A.D. It is flat, with two handles and is ornately decorated.

The consequences

Obviously this flood of prosperity brought change. At first small unnoticeable changes, then as the decades passed more obvious ones, transformed the society of the Romans who were now spread over the whole of Italy.

Some became excessively rich, even more so than the emperor who was still, however, in charge. Others completely stopped working. Such a large amount of grain arrived from Egypt that the state was able to distribute it almost free. On the peninsula and in Sicily which was Rome's ancient granary, the growing of cereals began to decrease. Others didn't work simply because they had slaves who worked for them. Some people used this 'otium', this abundance of free time, for study, learning foreign languages, or steeping themselves in art. But most of them passed their time in the huge banquets and ridiculous amusements and stupid exhibitions of luxury and riches. In short, the Empire provided riches and Rome began to drown in them. This was a slow process, obviously. But in the end the result was catastrophic. This was the diabolic mechanism that no-one knew how to stop.

Endless feasts

The Romans had always enjoyed a good feast. Even during the centuries of greatest hardship, each year had about 100 'feriae', or obligatory feast days.

These were usually religious feasts even if they often ended in joyful and exultant uproar. One of the largest was the feast of

In Imperial Rome more than 200 days a year were feast days, dedicated to games in the Circus and gladiator fights. The gladiators, who were often slaves, were trained to fight in public. There were various forms of combat: sometimes two gladiators fought against each other, or else they fought in groups; sometimes a gladiator even fought wild animals.

the Saturnalia; from the 17th to the 23rd of December in honour of the god Saturn, under whose remote reign it was rumoured that people had lived in a paradisal 'golden age'. After the holy sacrificial rites there was total freedom dedicated to complete enjoyment. It was the only occasion in the year in which the rigid distinction between masters and slaves not only didn't exist but was even reversed: the masters served their slaves and they even obeyed their orders. There were so many feast days that even the calendar was affected. At the beginning of every month the high priest called together the people and told them which were the feast days to be celebrated over the next 30 days. In ancient Latin this 'calling out' was called 'kalere' which has now passed to our word 'calendar'.

Sports and cruel games

To win the favour of the influential people of Rome some rich men began to organise free shows at the Circus or the amphitheatre on the occasion of some feast day or another. At first these were usually sports competitions, especially races with chariots pulled by two, four, eight or ten horses. Great excitement, cheering, whistling and applause accompanied these races. The 'support' for these competitions could only be compared to that seen during the World Cup in modern times. Later on these

games became a lot crueller: fights to the death between men, or with men against wild animals were common. All this just to amuse an ever more demanding and insatiable public.

In the end, to keep the people happy, the consuls, the Senate and the emperors were practically forced to multiply the feast days and increase this sort of spectacle. This was a terrible blow to the state finances.

The beginning of the end

Despite the lavish corruption that flourished in Rome, the empire continued to expand and reached its height c. A.D. 260 when its borders stretched from the North Sea to the Sahara Desert, and from the Black Sea to the Atlantic Ocean. But it was becoming more difficult to administer and in 285 the Emperor Diocletian divided it into two parts – an eastern empire and a western one. He promoted his old friend Maximian to be emperor of the eastern empire which carried on until 1453 when the Turks invaded its capital, Constantinople. But the western empire came to an end in 476 when Romulus Augustus was deposed.

However, by this time, Christianity had been adopted by many Roman citizens as their religion, and although the empire is long since dead, today Rome is the spiritual capital of Roman Catholicism, one of the most widespread of today's religions.

MEDICINE IN ROME

Under the Roman empire medicine also made great progress: medical associations ('collegia') sprang up, with doctors usually coming from Magna Grecia, Greece or the Hellenic East. These were the most expert at diagnosing illnesses and their cures were mostly made from natural medicines like herbs. There were also skilled surgeons who made use of highly efficient instruments to carry out delicate operations like amputations and the removal of teeth and tonsils. During Imperial times, a regular medical service was ordered for the army and among the fleet.

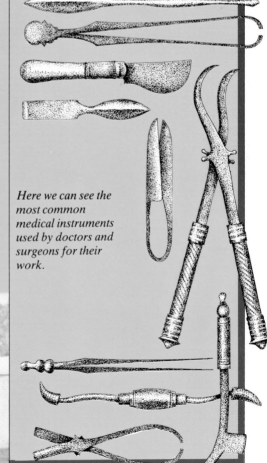

Here we can see the most common medical instruments used by doctors and surgeons for their work.

Index

Note: Page numbers in *italics* refer to illustrations.

Achaeans, 5, 6, 24
Acropolis, Athens, 12
Actium, battle of, 43; *42*
aediles *see* magistrates, Roman
Aegean Basin, 16; *7*
Aequines, 24, 33
Africa, Northern: and Greeks, 16; infantrymen, *36*; and Punic Wars, 37; and Romans, 33, 40
Agamemnon, King of Mycenae, 7
Albalonga, 23, 24
Alexander the Great, 18
Alexandria, 18
Ammon, 18
ancient rites and customs: Cretan, 2, 3, 4; Greek, 12, 13, 14; Roman, 23, 25, 47
Antonius, Marcus (Mark Antony), 43
Aosta, *41*
'Apella' *see* Assembly of Equals, Athens
Aphrodite, 13
'apoikia', 15
aqueducts, Roman, *40*
Archimedes' screw, *21*
Ares, 13
Argos, 6, 7
Aristarchus of Samos, 20
army, Roman, 29, 36, 40; *38–9*, *41*; *see also* legion and legionary
Asia Minor, 7, 16
Assembly, Athens, 8, 10
Assembly of Equals, Athens, 8
Athene, 13; *19*
Athens, 7; dominance of, 8, 12; government of, 10, 11; and ostracism, 11; and Philip II, King of Macedon, 18; society of, 10; and Sparta, 12
Attica, 10
Augustus, Emperor of Rome, 43, 45; *42*
Aurelius, Emperor of Rome, 24

Black Sea, 7, 16
bull jumping, 4

Caesar, Julius, 42–3; *42*
calendar, Roman, 47
Canuleian Tribunal, Rome, 31
Carthage, 16, 33, 34; and Rome, 34–5, 37, 40, 41
Celius, Rome *see* Lateran, Rome
Celts, 33
censors, Roman, 31
Centurial Assemblies, Rome, 29, 30, 31
centuries, Roman, 29
centurions, Roman *36*
Chaeronea, battle of, 18
chariot races, *13*
Circus Maximus, Rome, 26, 47; *44–5*
city state, *see* 'polis'
class system, Roman, 28, 29–30
Cleopatra, Queen of Egypt, 43
Clistenes, 10
Cloaca Maxima, Rome, 26
coins, Roman, *28*
consuls, Roman, 29, 31; *29*
Corinthian League, 18
Corsica, 34, 40
craftwork: Cretan, 3, 4, 5; Roman *46*

Crassus, 43
Crete, Cretans, 2–5, 7, 16
Curia, Rome, 31
Curial Assemblies, Rome, 30, 31
Cyclops, 7
Cyrene, 16; *17*

Darius, King of Persia, 18
democracy, foundation of, 10
Democritus, 20
dictators, Roman, 31
Dionysius, 13
Dorica, Dorians, 8, 9, 16
Dracon, 10
Duilius, Caius, 35

education, of Spartans, 9
'efori', 8
Egypt, 18
entertainment, Roman, 47
Eolide, 16
Epaminondas, Theban General, 13
Eratosthenes, 20
Etruscans, 22, 24, 26, 33
Euclid, 21

Forum, Rome, 25; *44–5*
France, 16

Gaugamela, battle of, 18
Gauls, *see* Celts
Ge, 13
geography and the Greeks, 20
gladiators, *47*
gods: Greek, 4, 12, 13, 24; *19*; Roman, 4, 22, 23, 24, 25, 45, 47
Granicus, battle of, 18
Great Greece, 16, 33
Greece: and Achaeans, 6, 7; civilisation, 6, 7; colonisation, 15, 16, 17, 24; and Crete, 5, 7, 16; cultural development, 19–21; dark age, 8; and Dorians, 8; and Persian Empire, 12, 18; and Punic Wars, 37; and Rome, 33, 41

Hannibal, 37; *36*
Hasdrubal, brother of Hannibal, 37
Helots, 9
Hermes of Veii, *26*
Heron of Alexandria, 20; his 'eolipila', *21*
hieroglyphics, 5
hoplites, 9
Hostilius, Tullus, King of Rome, 25
houses, Roman, 30

Ida, Mount, 4
Ilium, *see* Troy
India, 18
Indo-Europeans, 6, 8, 10; *7*
'insula' (Roman housing), 30
Ionia, Ionians, 10, 16
Italy: and Achaeans, 24; and Etruscans, 24; and Greeks, 16, 24; *17*; and Punic Wars, 37; and Romans, 33, 37, 45

Janus, 45
Jupiter, 4, 24, 25

'kalere' *see* calendar, Roman
Knossos, 3, 5; Royal Palace, 2, 3; *4*, *5*

Lateran, Rome, 25
Lateranus, Sextus, 31
Latin League, 33
Latium, Latins, 24, 33

Laurion, Mount, 10
law, Roman, 31
legion and legionary, Roman, 29, 36–7, 40; *32*, *36*
Lepidus, Marcus Aemilius, 43
Lucans, 22, 24
Luceres, 25, 26
Lucumo *see* Tarquin the Proud

Macedon, Macedonians, 18
magistrates, Roman, 28, 30, 31
'Magna Graecia' *see* Great Greece
Marathon, 12
Marcius, Ancus, King of Rome, 25, 26
Mars, 23
mathematics, and the Greeks, 21
medicine, Roman, 47
Mediterranean coast: and the Greeks, 16, 17; and the Romans, 33
'Meteci', 11
Minoan civilisation, 4
Mother Earth, 5, 23
Mycenae, Mycenaeans, 6, 7, 16; and Asia Minor, 7; civilisation, 7, 8; and the Dorians, 7; war with Troy, 7

Octavia, wife of Mark Antony, 43
Octavianus, Caius Julius Caesar (Octavian) *see* Augustus, Emperor of Rome
Olympia, 12
Olympiad, *see* Olympic Games
Olympias, Queen of Macedon, 18
Olympic Games, 4, 12; *13*
Olympus, Mount, 4
'opliti' *see* hoplites
ostracism, 11
'ostrakon', *11*
'otium', 47

Paestum, *see* Posidonia
Palatine, Rome, 22, 25; *23*, *44–5*
Pales, 22
Pantheon, Rome, *44–5*
'patres', Roman, 25, 26, 29
patricians, Roman, 30, 31
Pax Romana, 45–6
Peloponnese, 7, 8
Pericles, 12
Perieci, 9
Persian Empire, 12, 17, 18
Phalerum, 10
Philip II, King of Macedon, 18
Phoenicia, Phoenicians, 16, 18
Piraeus, 10, 12
plebs, Roman, 30
poetry, and the Greeks, 21
'polis', 8, 10, 18
Pompeii, electoral publicity at, *28*
Pompey, 43
Pompilius, Numa, King of Rome, 25
Pontus Euxinus *see* Black Sea
Poseidon, 13; temple to, *17*
Posidonia, *17*
praetors, Roman, 31, 45
'Prince of Lilies' (Cretan painting), *5*
Priscus, *see* Tarquin the Proud
'proletarii', Roman, 29
Punic Wars, 33–7
Pyrrhus, King of Epirus, 33
Pythagoras, 21

Qart-Hadasht, *see* Carthage
Quirinal, Rome, 25

Ramnes, 22, 23, 25, 26
Remus, 23
roads, Roman, *30*, *33*

Roman Empire, 33, 43–7
Rome: birth and early development, 22–3, 25; building boom, 45; and Carthage, 33, 34, 35; and the Etruscans, 26, 33; Imperial Rome, *24*, *44–5*; and Italy, 33, 34; Monarchical era, 25–7; *27*; Republic of Rome and its government, 27, 28–31; seven hills of, *24*; at war, 30, 32–41; wealth of, 46–7
Romulus, King of Rome, 22, 23, 25, 30
Rumulus, *see* Romulus

Sabines: in Latium, 24; and Rome, 22, 25
Samnites: in Latium, 24; and the Romans, 33
Sardinia, 34, 40
Saturn, 47
Saturnalia, feast of, 47
Scipio, Publius Cornelius, 37
sculpture: Greek, 21; Roman, *23*
Senate, Roman: structure of, 25, 26, 30; power of, 31
Senate House, Rome, 25
Senate House Assemblies, Rome, 25
senators, Roman, 31
'seniores', Roman, 25
ships, *see* warships
Sicily: and the Greeks, 16, 24; and the Punic Wars, 34, 37; and the Romans, 40
slaves: Greeks, 8, 11; Roman, 40, 46, 47
Solon, 10
Spain: and the Greeks, 16; and the Punic Wars, 37; and Rome, 33, 40
Sparta, Spartans, 8, 9, 12, 13; *14*
'Spartiati', 9
stele, funerary, *31*
Stolo, Lucinius, 31
Syria, 18, 24, 33, 37

Taigets, Mount, 9
Tarquin the Proud (Lucius Tarquinius), King of Rome, 26–7
Tatius, Titus, 25
theatre, Greek, 21; *20*
Thebes, 7, 12; and Sparta, 13; and the Macedonians, 18
Thera, 5
Tiber, River, 22, 23; *26*
Tiglath-pileser III, King of Syria, 24
Tiryns, 6, 7
Tities, 22, 25, 26
Treasury of Atreus, Mycenae, 7
Tribal Assemblies, Rome, 30, 31
Tribunes of the People, Rome, 31
triremes, 12, 14; *14–15*
Trojan War, 7, 16
Troy, 7
Tullius, Servius, King of Rome, 24, 26, 27
Turkey, 37
Twelve Tablets, 31
Tyre, siege of, 18

Ulysses, King of Ithaca, 7

Volsci, 24, 33

warships: Cretan, 3; Greek, 12; *14–15*; Roman, 34, 35

Yugoslavia, and the Punic Wars, 34, 37

Zeus, 4, 12, 13, 24